How to be I[...]
to the Opposite Sex

(The Art of Dating, Mating & Long Term Relating™)

Susan E. Bradley RN

A Life Changing Guide
to Loving

Lo♥ing University Press

Rather than give you multiple endorsements from other authors--listen to what readers have been saying about this book.

"I spent thousands of dollars on dating services with little results...until I changed my ultra conservative non-sensual look to the one found on page fifty-one of this book. Now, I'm more confident. Plenty of eligible men are vying for my attention."
Nadia Cleveland, Ohio

"I used the love and attraction strategies with my girlfriend. Now Laurie's my wife and the mother of our child."
John Cupple

"My wife and I were bored with our life and each other, until we used this book and it's companion guide. What a difference!"

"This book made my heart dance!"
Mary Baugh

"Susan, tells it like it is! Listen to her and you will get results."
Michael Cammarata Michigan

"My husband died after our 24th anniversary. I learned the information and confidence I needed to look for love again."
Annie Morrow

Giftstore, Bookstore & Mail Order Distribution
800-266-7284

Isbn -1-888670-30-4

Isbn for the accompanying 112 pg. Companion Guide:

Also known as *How to be Even More Irresistible* 1-888670-31-2

First Printing
Printed in the United States of America

10 9 8 7 6 5 4 3 2 1

Published by
Lo♥ing University ™ Press
P.O. Box 771133 Cleveland Ohio 44107 216-521-Love (5683)
E-mail: LovingUniv@aol.com

Leg Photography by S. Bradley
Illustrations by Dennis Thorton Maui, Hawaii 808-877-3592

Publisher's Cataloging in Publication Data
Bradley, Susan E., 1957–
How to be Irresistible to the Opposite Sex

1. Relationships 2. Psychology 3. Self-help 4. How-to

Library of Congress Catalog Number-95-95352

ISBN-1-888670-30-4

About the Author

Susan Bradley was born the day *Love Letters in the Sand* was the number one song. So, it's no coincidence that she is now considered a pioneer in the study of relationships. Her approach to relationship building has been called magical, inspirational, and practical. She is a Registered Nurse, Clinical Hypnotherapist, Trainer in Neuro-Linguistic Programming, Relationship Coach and hosts her own Relationship Talk Show; Dating♥Mating♥LongTerm Relating™.

As the founder of Loving University ™, she believes that the secret of creating your life occurs relationship by relationship. Additionally, Loving University is committed to decreasing the divorce rate by increasing the number of healthy marriages through teaching others how to love. Susan Bradley has coached thousands.

Perhaps, she can help you.

Loving University ♥
216-521-Love (5683)
P.O. Box 771133 Cleveland OH 44107

Business clients, such as: U.S. Veterans Hospitals, Ohio Bell (Ameritech), Keane Inc., and many other organizations rely on her to produce results by presenting complex information in a practical, concise, and uncomplicated manner.

Because of her ability to create shifts in effectiveness, she is a highly sought after spokesperson for key note addresses, conventions, and meetings. Companies consider her their secret weapon in teaching their staff superior relating skills.

Susan appears on TV/Radio shows nationwide and is a columnist for singles magazines nationwide: *Ohio's Finest Singles*, Pittsburgh's *Lifestyle*, and *Single Connections* (Chicago). *Ohio Magazine* called her "the gentle generalissimo." The *Cleveland Plain Dealer*--"the Love Coach." Her consultant relationship with Great Expectations (a national video dating service) also provided a wealth of insights and research on single life.

Member: National Speakers Association
American Association of Occupational Health Nurses

Susan Bradley resides in Cleveland, Ohio with her awesome daughter, Ariana and lifepartner, Jon.

Look for the upcoming titles by Susan Bradley: "The Journey Into Love," and "The Secret of Creating Your Life - Relationship by Relationship," "When Women Speak in Estrogen, Men speak in Testosterone," "Flirting With Greatness," and "FamilyQuest™."

CONTENTS

II. MATING-Rituals of Courtship & Compatibility

III. RELATING

Acknowledgments

First let me thank the many mentors and teachers of my life. . . My grandmothers, who taught me how to love. . . Mrs. Sites, who taught me to believe in my abilities and dream big dreams. . . Mom and Dad, who had the foresight to spend their hard earned dollars on traveling and meeting people all over the country. Mom, who made sure that "I got religion."

Many people led me to my path of enlightenment, and for that I am so grateful. Robert Panté, Anthony Robbins, Tad James, Richard Bandler, Barbara DeAngelis Ph.D., Marianne Williamson, Wayne Dyer. These people I have been fortunate to meet and/or get significant coaching from.

Some of you I've had the pleasure of meeting via my radio talk show and we've connected for a moment: Dr. Bernie Siegel, John Gray Ph.D., Dr. Patricia Love, Melody Beattie. Many others may not be mentioned but their books and seminars helped create my life and guide me to my purpose.

Without the support, love and encouragement in the wee hours of the night from my closest friends. . . Lisa Fosdick-Biggers, Dr. Joel Rossen, Marcea Lovejoy, Marcia Minor, and Joyce Krost. . . this book would have never happened.

To the men in my life (you know who you are): Thank you for the lessons of love and life that we experienced together.

Almost last, but not least, my daughter Ariana, who has perhaps sacrificed and tolerated the most. You repeatedly understood when mom stayed up all night writing and was cranky the next day, or went away from you for a week at a time to seminars and left you in the loving care of others. You are a gift to me, Ariana. You light up my life with your compassion for myself and others.

Jon, my loving partner in life: I thank you for your generous gift of time, love, and support in this process. As Bette Midler so aptly wrote, "You are the wind beneath my wings."

Technically speaking. . . Pat Murray, you were my detail oriented wordsmith who taught me that when you have clarity with your words you will have clarity in your life. Audrey Katzman, my editor-in-chief, thank you for allowing my own personal style of speaking through writing to shine with the appropriate commas and emphasis. Gloria Goddess, you truly are. . . Thank you.

Being *IRRESISTIBLE*
starts with a decision.

It shows up in attitude
and creates an expectation. . .

Think about what you consider *irresistible* in your life. . . Is it the thought of a full body massage. . . an all expense paid vacation on a island. . . a hot fudge sundae. . . peace of mind? Men might imagine that irresistible would be having an unlimited supply of sexual experiences. For women it might seem irresistible to imagine a man with all of their ideal romantic qualities. . . a knight in shining armor.

For some people, the word "irresistible" conjures up ideas of fantasy. . . pipe dreams. . . following your own *journey to love*. . . so that whatever previously seemed unattainable or unreachable begins to appear in your life.

You may not even believe that being irresistible is something you can do, but try it on like a new suit or an evening dress. Close your eyes and imagine that you have no emotional baggage. . . you've never been hurt in any of your relationships. . . not by your mother or your father or anyone else. . . Imagine that you could trust everyone in your life, including yourself, to do what is right for you. Close your eyes and do that now. . . Really imagine it.

Now see yourself erasing negative memories from your past but keeping any learning or lessons. Create an irresistible smile on your face. . . Did you ever hear someone laugh so hard that it made you laugh and you didn't even know why you were laughing? That's irresistible. Did you ever want to hold a baby bird or kitten in your hand just for an instant? That's irresistible. Did you ever admire a flower so much that you wanted to pick it? That's _____!

Did you ever see someone and you just knew that you wanted a relationship with them? What stopped you from having that relationship? Did you ever talk to them? No? Well, it's time for some new skills. . .

Becoming *irresistible* to someone else begins with being *irresistible* to yourself and creating an irresistible life. . .Laughing at your own jokes, enjoying your talents and gifts, expressing yourself with a positive visual image and body language, being proud of yourself and the personal growth you have accomplished, and knowing that you are doing the best job that you can.

Whether you feel you have a long way to go or just a short distance. . . Relax! Realize that while creating an irresistible life won't happen over night, you can decide to begin NOW. Begin by ordering a free copy of *30 Ways to Have 30 Days of Love in your Life* (found in the Companion Guide of *How to be Irresistible*, if you have already purchased it). I recently received a letter about *30 Days* from a woman in Southern Ohio, who wrote, "I love it! 60 days ago I had no man. . . now I have 3 and one is a good possibility. Thank you, thank you!"

Becoming irresistible will begin to happen when you put what you've learned about yourself and others into practice. Try the entire book and tape course "How to Be Irresistible to the Opposite SEX!" (For the book, workbook, and audiotape, call 1-800-Compatible 1-800-266-7284.) It will take you on a journey to having an irresistible life filled with incredible relationships. . . It will ask you to try on new thoughts and ideas. If you keep on doing what you've always done. . . you'll get the same results that you now have. If that's what you want, great! Otherwise, reassess where you are and what you want to accomplish in the area of relationships. Every one is different, with different needs.

You will learn about the fundamentals of **Dating ♥Mating♥ LongTerm Relating**. . . you'll enjoy the humor. . . you'll enjoy the truth and the insights. . . and you will become *irresistible.*

INTRODUCTION

The beginning of any relationship seems pretty irresistible. I, like many of you, have experienced the exhilaration of many relationships that fizzled in three months. I remember too many dateless nights wondering what was wrong. Why didn't I have someone special in my life? I was attractive, intelligent and loving. Heck, I supported and coached one of my best friends, Lisa and her twin sister into marriages. When was it going to happen for me?

I've been engaged twice, married and divorced, and proposed to at least five times. I've spent more years single and dating than married. I think I personally have experienced almost every type of dating experience, good and bad: long distance relationships, phone relationships, on-line relationships, short to longer relationships, sexual relationships, friend relationships, co-dependent relationships, etc., etc. You name it, I've tried it.

I spent ten years after my divorce healing, learning and growing into the person I now am. I would not have been ready to have the relationship that I now have with my lifepartner, Jon ,without the preparation time. I guess one decade was worth the investment to find someone to explore life with for the next five decades.

My life has given me a multitude of personal experiences to share, as well as the collective experiences of all of the friends, clients, and seminar participants that I have coached over the last decade. I believe that my purpose in life is to support and coach other people in achieving happiness through accepting themselves, their sexuality and the desire to connect with a partner in life.

HEAL ME, GUIDE ME, TEACH ME, LEAD ME

You're walking around on emotional crutches. . . if you fall to pieces when someone looks at you funny. . . or doesn't ask you out for another date. . . if you make it mean all kinds of derogatory things, like: "I'm not good enough." Or, "I should have worn different clothes." Or, "I'll never succeed." "They don't believe in me."

As a nurse for over 18 years, I have personally seen people believe that they would recover and DO IT! I remember one man who was crushed between two trains, survived, and eventually walked again. Why? Because he didn't listen to the people who told him it wasn't possible. He listened to himself. My patients have taught me more over the years than I can ever tell you.

Now I am a faith healer for relationships. I want to make believers out of all of you! I want to take away your crutches and let you see that you can live your life fully and passionately, and that you do not have to conform to everyone else's wishes. I want to give you permission to go for every gift that life has to offer. Why not? You deserve it!

Some people may say, "Who are you to want and have everything in life?" I want you to have it all! But first, you must believe it yourself and believe in yourself. Believe in love and life!

I want you to have total and complete belief in who you are. Humanity has lost faith in itself. Nearly every week I hear about men who commit suicide because they believe their families would be better off without them. My own grandfather and Jon's mother made that decision too. Where does that despair come from? When did they stop believing in themselves? Why didn't they learn to value themselves as unique, loving, human beings with something to contribute?

What would you do differently in life if you *truly* believed in yourself, if you really started to see yourself as the miracle that you already are? I challenge you turn to the person sitting next to you now and say, "You know, I'm simply irresistible!" Would you be able to tell that to anyone? How about to yourself? If you can't say that about yourself, who will?

Being **irresistible** is about that: believing that you deserve the best quality toilet paper. . . that you to deserve to order what you really want on a menu. . . that you deserve to decorate your house in a way that makes you happy and fully self-expressed. . . that you deserve to wear an outrageous hat without fearing ridicule, and deserve to love and be loved.

I am a faith healer, and the faith I want you to regain is in yourself and your value as an **irresistible** contribution to yourself and the world around you. Your life is created relationship by relationship. If you have no significant relationship, then you need to create that relationship with yourself. Your parents gave you the first chance to become a person by getting together and conceiving you. After that moment, it is, and always was, up to you.

Your relationships are a mirror, an exact replica of what you think and believe about yourself. When you look at a man or woman from across the room and decide instantaneously that you are not interested in them, you are giving others permission to judge and evaluate you in the same way. When you blame others for not accepting you, you condemn yourself. But, when you admit that you love your life even when every area of it is not perfect, you open a window for love to come to you.

Many re-singled people achingly wonder when and if they will ever find someone special again until it happens. Still, I ask my clients, "Are you sure you want a relationship? They are not easy." People who have been single for a long time don't remember what it takes to grow and compromise when they are sharing their daily life and responsibilities with another human being. They often forget the challenges that occurs when men speak in testosterone and women in estrogen. Nevertheless, we still crave that connection to another warm and loving being.

Do you think that finding the perfect lover and partner in life will fix everything? Ask anyone who's been married and divorced and they'll tell you that that's not the way it works. A fulfilling relationship will not happen to you if you just wander around mumbling, "I'm ready for a relationship. I'm ready for a relationship." **You need to *be* ready and *get* ready.**

Some people will tell you that you need to be more assertive. Others say, "Get more confidence." Where does one go to learn confidence? What is confidence? Belief! Belief and faith in yourself. How will you get that? By making mistakes. . . by getting out of the locker room and onto the playing field. . . by giving yourself permission to fall down in your day-to-day life, then getting back up, dusting yourself off, and trying again.

So, Mr. Right doesn't call you back after the third date. Who cares? Get right back out there again. He probably was doing you a favor. So why are you moping around about it and giving his actions meaning?

So, Ms. Right doesn't give you her phone number the first time you ask her. What does that really mean? You're unlovable? Not! It means you need to get out of the locker room with your antiseptic bandages, bleeding heart, and hurt feelings, to discover someone who will find you **irresistible!**

Warning: It won't happen until you begin creating an irresistible life with the most irresistible person in it: YOU!

Look around you, put out your arms and say, "Heal me! Guide me! Teach me! Lead me! Lead me to love and accept myself. Show me a way to have passionate, fulfilling relationships."

READ THIS BOOK AND DO WHAT IT SAYS!

My goal in creating this book is to provide a reusable resource that will improve your ability to relate with the opposite sex. The emphasis is practical rather than theoretical. In other words, you will learn to "walk your talk." Just reading *How to Be Irresistible* won't guarantee that you'll have more satisfying relationships. I want you to have an incredible relationship, but simply being aware of these skills isn't going to help you unless you actually put the ideas to work.

Like any skill, such as playing the piano or learning to golf, true expertise takes consistent effort over time. While you can learn a lot in a one-day seminar or by reading a book, you must get out of the locker room and onto the playing field to achieve your goals. As you learn and practice the skills discussed on the following pages, you can expect to pass through four stages.

The first stage in learning any new skill is a beginning awareness that there is a better way of doing things. Reading this book should bring this awareness to you.

The second stage requires stepping out of your comfort zone and trying out new love-attracting skills. Do you remember how awkward you were when you first tried to ride a bicycle or learned how to drive a stickshift car? You may feel a bit awkward at times as you stretch and grow while creating an irresistible relationship.

In the third stage of practicing these new skills, the discomfort of your initial attempts will begin to disappear. At this point, you will have created a new comfort level and the results will start to show. The more you practice, the more automatic your new behaviors and beliefs will become.

The fourth stage brings about unconscious competence. You will create a certain level of healthy expectations about love and what I call "REALationships." Don't let this feeling of achievement blind you from adding new loving skills and from reality checks on the status of your personal growth and development of your sexuality.

It's important to keep these four stages in mind as you try these concepts on for size. Prepare yourself for the inevitable uneasiness of stepping out into a new comfort zone. Learning and practicing the skills introduced here can help virtually every reader create more successful relationships. You will become irresistible to the opposite sex when these new-found abilities become second nature to you. I am convinced that these skills will work as long as you are willing to put in the time necessary to learn them.

If you are married and reading this book, it will help you and your partner learn more about each other and be able to short-circuit any negative patterns you may have fallen into. You'll create a deeper more fulfilling relationship. You'll learn how to love your partner in such a way that he or she naturally wants you to have everything you want and vice versa. Do the surveys and techniques found here and in the companion guide together. Share this book with friends, and you'll find that the more you share, the more you will integrate what you are learning and become an expert yourself.

I don't know when your perfect partner will appear in your life, when your current partner will be "perfect" for you, or how many people you will need to date before you find "the one." Finding love cannot be hurried — it's a process. But, if you are in a hurry, read through this book quickly and try things out. Then, go back and re-read and spend more time on each of the suggestions.

Whatever your situation is. . . I wish you a pleasant journey into love!

I'm fifty three years old and six foot four.

I've had three wives, five children,

and three grandchildren.

I love good whiskey. I still don't understand
women, and I

don't think there is any man who does.

-- John Wayne

Ŧop Ŧen ℂWorst Excuses for Ŋot ℂDating

10. I'm just too busy. (Would you be too busy to redeem the winning lottery ticket?)

9. I'm waiting for the right person to come along.

8. I want to lose 20 pounds first. (Sure, sure!)

7. The good ones are all married. (Or, there's no one good left.)

6. All men/women are jerks.

5. I'm shy. (There are a lot of shy married people. They dated too!)

4. I'm waiting until my kids are grown. (By that time, you may be overwhelmingly out of practice in relating to the opposite sex.)

3. I'm not ready yet. (If you are recently divorced give yourself around two years to heal, get your life together, and discover yourself. If you are out of a relatively short relationship give yourself two months maximum.) If you wait until you think and feel you are ready, it may be a lifetime.

2. I've been hurt too many times before. (Who hasn't?) What if your mother wouldn't let you learn to walk because you fell down too many times? Enough said.

1. It's too much work. (So are your job, house, children, but you find them necessary and worthwhile.)

No Time and Effort Invested = No Gain.

A Mate is a Permanent Type of Date!

Susan Bradley

Relationship Saving Technique

When you have been in a committed relationship for a while, it's easy to take each other for granted. You may settle in and be tempted to give less attention to the health of your relationship.

When you are dating, you aim to please. You automatically try harder to please so that your date will prefer to spend more time getting to know you over someone else.

So, when problems occur and you begin to think that you can't tolerate your partner for another minute try the lottery technique or the dating technique.

Lottery Technique: Pretend that they have just won the lottery and you want them to share it with you.

Dating Technique: Pretend that you have just met and only behave in a way that you would with a new partner. Pretend that you are out on a first date no matter how aggravating the situation is.

Chapter One

Why You Should Read This Book

This book is for you and anyone else you know who has ever suffered from not feeling absolutely loved, a book for those who have known the pain of loss, loneliness, or regret in relationships. Here you'll find a collection of information and a new resource to support and fine-tune your relationship skills. No matter how successful you feel you are or aren't in this arena, you'll benefit from this book's reminders.

This book is for: All the men who have come home to find their wife, family and belongings gone; the women who tried to be loved and understood until they tried no more; and for all of you who are out of practice in finding a loving life partner.

If love has ever confused you or eluded you, begin to change that now. Keep reading. Identify the areas where your relationships need the most support, resources, new skills, and new information, then apply the concepts found in chapters 1-26. Use the companion guide to learn more about what you really want in your life. Don't miss the challenging belief technique in the Companion Guide that erases the pain of rejection.

- This book is a collection of skills, exercises and relationship techniques. Feel free to read it out of sequence. Just use the Table of Contents to find the areas you wish to focus on and return later to read the rest.

- Read this book if you do not have a relationship or you want to magically transform your current relationship.

- If you are not sure that you really want a relationship take a look at the following:

FACT: A great career can't fill the void of loneliness we feel when we have no one to share our life with.

FACT: We spend more time and money on our careers than on our love life. We go to college or technical schools to support our career choices. We attend seminars, conferences, meetings, etc. We read books, get hands-on experience, do things we don't want to do, put in overtime, etc.

Remember:

No Investment = No Returns.

FACT: Our parents didn't teach us how to create fabulous, fulfilling relationships. They taught us how to ride a bike, tie our shoes, have good manners, and do well in school, but they never directed our attention to relationship skills.

For all of the above reasons and more,

you need to fill in the missing

links in your relating skills.

FACT: You will learn superior relationship skills in this book and it will be easier than you think.

Yet, take note. Sometimes trying out a new skill, can feel like this: You're swinging out on a trapeze. You let go — you're suspended in mid air and there's no trapeze in sight. Don't panic, the trapeze will come. If you are willing to "hang out" in this space you will emerge stronger than before and be on your way to finding that loving, healing, nurturing relationship that you deserve.

FACT: A fabulous relationship can ease the misery of most circumstances in life. A miserable relationship can be torture.

FACT: A great career may keep us occupied, but it can't keep us company in our old age, be there for us during sickness and health, or encourage us to keep going when the outlook is bleak.

FACT: This book is the beginning of a great journey into the world of relationships. To begin that journey, start at chapter three; for those in doubt, read chapter two.

Chapter Two

How to stay *single or married* and *unloved* the rest of your life.

DO NOT read this book.

Go watch TV instead.

Actions, not words, are the true criteria of the attachment of friends.

-- *George Washington*

Top Seven Dating Tips

1. Make the first three dates after your first meeting very special (a dressy date, one fun casual date, and one semi-dressy).

2. Call no sooner than 36 hours after the first date and no later than three days to say you had a great time. **Note:** Wait another 8-24 hours and call again for your next date.

3. Focus on FUN. Keep discussions lively, interesting and light.Do not discuss past relationships, parents, religion or politics on the first date. When asked about previous relationships, simply mention when it was, how long it lasted; then, change the subject.

4. Use dating to expand your mind, learn new hobbies, lose weight, learn about art or music, learn how to play backgammon or cook gourmet, exercise, try new foods and restaurants. Pick each other's minds and become resources to one another. Learn to dance or appreciate sports. Go to lectures or exhibits together — you'll have something automatically ready to talk about.

5. Plan on spending six months just dating different people to get a real feel for what you do or don't want in a relationship. Keep more eggs in your basket for a while until you are sure that you want to explore one of the potentials for a longer period of time.

6. Dress sensuously but appropriately. **Men:** forget your extra-comfy clothes and show women how good you clean up. **Women:** Try heels, lipstick, and v-neck tops.

7. **Re: blind dates and first meetings: Men: If you really like her and want to see her again, pay for the date! It's a sign you are interested. Women: If you are not interested in seeing him again, offer to pay for your portion. Some men will accept and some will prefer to pay.** (Those born before 1960 may still feel that the male should pay for the first three dates. Note: If he tells you something like, "I took you out, now put out," drop him like a hot potato. He's done you a favor by revealing his true nature.)

Dating

(The Dance Towards Intimacy)

Whatever you do
to <u>find</u> a relationship,
you must continue doing
to <u>keep</u> a relationship.

And it was Robert Frost
who once said,
"Everyone's most irresistible desire
is to be irresistibly desired!"

Top Ten Ways to Avoid Rejection

10. Learn to say one four-lettered word : N-E-X-T! Then, try, try again.

9. Practice saying, "That was good practice."

8. Do not consider yourself rejected unless s/he says something like, "Get out of my face, nerd-breath!"

7. Say to yourself: "I'm wonderful, I'm smart, and I never, never, give up." (Winston Churchill used to say something like this, too.)

6. My mother always told me "Many true words are spoken in jest." I believe my mother (you should, too). Never underestimate the power of using humor. Imagine the person who just turned you down wearing a neon muumuu, curlers in her hair, and mud masque all over her face. Don't forget to picture the food debris caught between her braces. There now, feel better?

5. If you've been turned down by a man: imagine him sitting on a stool with gum on his nose and a dunce cap on his head. Don't forget the bib with food dribbled on it. You didn't really want him anyway, did you?

4. Eat chocolate. . . lots of it. (Not a healthy alternative but definitely a delicious one.)

3. Remember that when someone doesn't choose you, they are merely stating a preference. S/he may have wanted strawberry and you are vanilla. It's no big deal.

2. Bone up on flirting skills and go for it again !

1. Don't stop until someone says, "YES!"

Chapter Three

In the Beginning, There was *Dating*

Everyone can have a successful relationship. In fact, many of you have already had successful relationships. They were **all** successful in the beginning, right? *The trick is to learn new skills to start those relationships on a better foundation and thereby make the successful part last longer. This work doesn't just begin the moment we meet someone. Preparation is a key to success.*
Some people need to overcome their shyness, anger, or fear of rejection. Other people need to learn how to value themselves more (and some, a little less). Everyone has different skill levels and experiences, so the preparation time is different.

While everyone has some obstacle to overcome in the journey to love, I have found that we all need practice and reminders on understanding gender differences. Begin by considering this familiar scenario:

In the beginning, there was man and woman. They first saw each other from across the horizon (or was it in a garden?). Their eyes locked, and it was love at first sight. But when he asked her to dance, she said, "Not now, maybe later." What did he hear? "Get lost!"

Feeling a sense of relief, he learned to say, "Next!" His eye caught yet another woman. Determined to do it right this time, he rushed to her side, bent on one knee and blurted out "Would you wind dancing mith we?" The woman, noticing how nervous and sincere he was, overlooked his bumbling attempt to woo her and responded with a smiling, "Yes!"

Can men and women ever truly understand each other? Yes, of course! If we imagine that **women speak in estrogen and men in testosterone**, we can listen to and interpret each other differently. First, pretend you're visiting another country where people speak a different language (you wouldn't go to France or Italy and expect everyone to speak English, would you?). It sounds similar to your country's native language, perhaps, but when you talk, it seems as though you have different meanings for the same words.

Even when languages are translated, we often do not make exact translations. For example: the word "shy" in French is *"timide."* This word is very close to our "timid," which not only means "shy," but indicates someone who doesn't speak up for him/herself.

Below are some examples of messages lost in translation when estrogen and testosterone attempt to communicate.

Example 1: She says: "Honey, I'm sick of this mess!" He hears, "You made this mess." What she means is: "Gee, I'm awfully tired of coming home to the same boring chores." She may not be blaming at all, but the male to whom she is speaking automatically interprets it this way. All the female wants to do is express how she feels so she can air out her feelings; then, she can work out a solution. Thus, the politically correct response for the male would be: "I know what you mean; what can we do about it?" This allows the female to vent more freely because she feels understood, and most likely she will come up with her own solution.

Example 2: He says: "I can't take this anymore, I'll see you later." She hears: "I'm leaving you!" He means: "I want to sort this problem out myself. I'll be back later."

These examples clearly show how different we really are, and how easy it is to create trouble spots in our relationships.

Important!:

There are differences

between the sexes.

Use them to your advantage.

For example, women don't really understand why men have the "sports gene," but if they learn to live with it they could use that time to pursue their own interests. Men, on the other hand, don't quite understand the "shopping gene," either; but the best equivalent I can give you is: think of it as a sport — the female sport of choice.

Speaking of sports, here's another comparison: The Super Bowl = The Giant Designer Clothing Sale. In other words, men enjoy the Super Bowl in much the same way women enjoy the challenge of finding the perfect dress or home decoration at a bargain price. Many women are as passionate about their homes as men are about their cars. Watch a man as he admires his favorite car: how he touches it, thinks about it, dreams about it, and talks about it. Listen to a woman as she describes what she wants to do next with her house.

Madam, I have been looking for a person who dislikes gravy all my life, let us swear eternal friendship.

-- Sydney Smith

Reprove a friend in secret but praise him before others.

-- Leonardo da Vinci

Top Seven Best Places To Find a Quality Male

1. Get involved in the Big Brother program and get to know the men who volunteer.

2. Work a part-time job in a men's clothing store , golf course, boating store or sporting goods store.

3. At the supermarket: ask him for advice, directions to the soup section, or what his favorite brand of _____ (any product that is close by) is, or if he's ever tried that particular brand of _____(whatever he's got in his cart).

4. At the local airport's "Cheers" bar, you'll meet locals waiting for a flight as well as interesting business travelers in-between flights.

5. Go to the lobby bar of the classiest hotels. Sit in a visible place without girlfriends, and smile at the men who appeal to you. Warning: be sure to avoid the ones that are only single when they are out of town.

6. Seminars and workshops of all kinds. Personal growth seminars are the best.

7. Church or synagogue.

Dating Etiquette:
What's In/What's Out

IN   Writing a note or leaving a message on the answering machine (even if you only went out once) to say you are no longer interested. Or be extra courageous and tell the person yourself.

      OUT   Not returning phone calls as a way of saying good-bye.

IN   Opening doors: **Women:** since men are not sure who might or might not want her door opened, pause for a minute at a door so he gets his cue. In a car, remain in your seat until he has a chance to get to your side.

      OUT   Chastising a woman for not letting you open the door.

IN   Going somewhere special for the first three dates.

      OUT   Just going for "coffee" if you're meeting for the first time, unless it's at a gourmet coffee house or one with a bookstore nearby. (Bookstores are well-known as great gathering places.) Try a boat/car/flower/art show where you can walk and talk and get to know each other's passions and preferences.

IN   Letting him/her know in the beginning if you have children.

      OUT   Talking negatively or incessantly about a former spouse or significant other. This kind of talk can't help but show your negative side, even if your "ex" was a real creep.

IN   Thanking your date for an enjoyable time within 24 - 48 hours. Keep it simple; don't go on and on. (This is not the time to ask for another date.)

      OUT   Flirting with the waitress (or anyone else) when you are out with a date!

Top 11 Ways to Guarantee You'll Never Get a Second Date

1. Discuss past significant others and tell your current dates how you're going to get even with them.

2. Show up on the first date wearing a plaid flannel shirt or looking like a college student on spring break. Seriously, men: it's one of women's biggest complaints. If a woman cannot proudly introduce you to her friends, you won't get past first base.

3. Ask him how much money he makes. I heard of one woman who asked on the first phone conversation, "How much money do you make in one hour ?" I'd run away screaming if I were you.

4. Start calling him/her every single day or several times a day because you miss him/her already.

5. Be rude to a waiter or waitress.

6. Try to have sex on the first date.

7. Start talking about how lonely your life is.

8. Take her to Hooters (or even more tasteless, to a topless bar.)

9. Discuss how many children you want to have.

10. Start lecturing or trying to improve your date.

11. Ask, "Where is this relationship going?"

Chapter Four

Swarming:
Birds Do It, Bees Do It.
Maybe You Should, Too!

A swarm of bees, a school of fish, a flock of birds: What do they know that we don't? They practice "swarming." Once you try this idea, you'll never forget it. Would you go fishing in a lake that only had three fish — even if they were big ones? Or would you find a lake that had lots of big fish? Would a hunter go to a forest that had only five bears? Or would he go where animals are traveling in packs? How much more honey would you get from 100 bees, as opposed to 10?

The Most Important Lesson
In Meeting Someone Special

Many people say, "I want a new job, a perfect relationship, or a special home," but then neglect to put themselves in situations that offer many choices. They need to "swarm."

If you go hunting where there is a crowd of jobs or potential mates, and someone turns you down, you can just say, "Okay, NEXT!" In other words, you won't have time to take it personally or feel rejected. If you "swarm," you'll have many choices. When you search in an area of high concentration, the next opportunity will always be nearby.

For example: If you want to live in a place that's right for you, you wouldn't look in an area that didn't qualify. You would search the papers, ask friends, and drive down streets of favored areas. Wouldn't you look at more than five places before you made up your mind? If you wanted the perfect job, wouldn't you answer lots of qualified ads, submit applications, and go to cities where there were more job opportunities? The same goes for relationships. So why do so many smart people who want a relationship avoid going to the right places, talking to others, answering ads, joining dating services, or creating a swarm of people to choose from?

The next step. Once you begin swarming, and surround yourself with a high concentration of potential mates, be prepared to make some intelligent choices.

Follow these key concepts to get the most out of swarming:

1. Swarm with groups of quality people; you'll want **quality** and **quantity**!

    A. Go out and socialize often. If you're a skier, ski with a group; if you are interested in music, go to concerts, etc.

    B. Give singles' ads and dating services a try. (See Chapter Ten for tips on choosing the best dating service.)

    C. Be willing to go out with a wide range and variety of people and do a "test drive" before you buy.

    D. Improve your flirting skills and turn on some irresistible charm. (See Chapter Nine.)

2. Look for qualities you find desirable, and keep an open mind. (For instance, a female accountant might not initially be attracted to a machinist, fearing that their lives may seem too different. Try to look beyond obstacles and stereotypes like these. Blue collar and white collar don't have to stay segregated.)

3. Get to know yourself better. What are your goals and aspirations?

4. Read, read, read! (See the *How to be Irresistible Companion Guide* for lists of suggested books and tapes.)

5. Improve your image. Dress to attract the kind of person you want and then keep him/her interested and attracted. Men: try silk shirts, colorful sweaters and ties. **Purple** and **teal** are the top two colors women like to see on men.

6.   Put time and energy into getting what you want.

**Use the concept of "swarming"
and you will find someone special!**

    I can promise that it will happen. The number of people you'll meet and learn from will be up to you. The results will equal the amount of determination, interest and effort you put forth. May your first "swarming experience" be a fun-filled adventure!

If you knew for sure that after meeting 101 men or women

in a 2 year period and getting your heart broken 4 times (or more),

that you would fall in love with someone you could spend the rest of

your life with, wouldn't you try, try, again?

S. E. B.

Macho Jake

Ernie a Nice Guy But ...

Chapter Five

Are YOU an NGB?

(Nice Guy/Gal But. . .)

To find out if the opposite sex is passing you by and why, read on and take the NGB survey. NGB's usually do not make it past the second or third date. Some will never make it to the first date. How many times have you heard people say things like:

> *Bob's such a nice guy, but. . . He's just not my type. Oh I don't know, there isn't anything wrong with him. He treats me well, he's polite, friendly . . . I guess there just isn't enough "chemistry."*

-- OR --

> *My girlfriend, Jean, is okay. But every time I ask her out it always has to be* me *deciding what to do. If I asked her how she felt about going to a movie, she'd say, "That's fine." Or if I asked her if she wanted to go to a game this weekend, she'd say, "That's fine." Where to eat? "Whatever you pick is just fine." It made me want to ask her to bungee jump just to hear her say, "That's fine."*

Bob and Jean were just "nice" people who went along with the crowd, never wished to seem demanding and thought it was respectful to let their dates choose what to do. **What was missing? Pizzazz**, active participation, decisiveness. Their partners or dates felt as if they were doing all the "work," all the planning, and all the organizing. They felt as if they were leading their partner around by the nose. This dooms the relationship quickly.

Why does this happen? Many women seem to prefer the more "macho" guy (who may not treat them well), because typical macho qualities create a sense of mystery and chemistry. Nice guys are too predictable when compared to the "macho type." Due to the perceived lack of chemistry, women lose interest. So what can NGB's do?

Don't fret. I'm not suggesting that you become a Marlon Brando or Al Pacino or Steven Segal. Female NGB's (Nice Girls But) do not need to imitate Marilyn Monroe, Raquel Welch, or "Pretty Woman." First, take this survey to find out if you are an NGB.

NGB Survey

Answer true or false to the following statements.

__1.   People tell you how "nice" you are.

__2.   While you're out on a date, you try too hard to please. (For example, *if you're a man*: opening doors, pulling out chairs, and bringing the car around is *à propos*. NGB's, on the other hand are overly attentive, flatter excessively, and relate their entire life history in the first phone conversation, leaving little left for further conversations. *If you're a woman*: you always order the least expensive item on the menu, talk too much, or are always to eager to do something "nice" for your date.)

__3.   You are an average dresser who wears conservative clothes instead of those that are "fun" or "interesting" (conservative examples: sweaters that are plain, solid, or two-toned, flannel plaid shirts in traditional colors). Average dressers never want to offend anyone nor stand out in a crowd.

__4.   You have worn the same hairstyle for the last 2-5 yrs. Some people haven't changed hairstyles since high school!

___5. You consider yourself shy (e.g. you experience uncomfortable periods of silence just after being introduced and/or wait for others to introduce themselves first).

___6. You are short or slightly overweight and are uncomfortable about that. (Who isn't? The key word here is "uncomfortable.")

___7. **Women:** You wear very little makeup or perfume. (You are so uncomfortable about wearing too much that you go to the opposite extreme. *Tip:* Always enhance your eyes and lips; skimp on foundation and blush if necessary.) **Men:** You seldom ask a woman out for a date the first time you meet.

___8. You do not like to flirt at all. (You are shy, nervous, concerned that you won't be taken seriously, or worried that you will look too "easy.")

___9. You rarely ask for what you really want. (You always allow your date to decide which movie to see or which restaurant to go to. Meanwhile, you hope that you'll get your turn but never ask.) This is self-defeating.

___10. When a waiter asks if you like your meal, you don't complain or send anything back, even if the food is cold or has a hair in it.

**So, how did you do?
Answering "true" to seven
or more questions means
*you could be an NGB.***

If you are an NGB, take heart. NGB's can be great people to date. In fact, non-NGB's or ANGB's (Almost NGB's) could be making a *big* mistake by not considering an NGB for a long term relationship. NGB's are loyal, trusting, predictable, caring, giving, usually open-minded to their potential mates, generous, helpful, and are willing to change and grow to please others. However, they are *not* daring, exciting, mysterious, flirtatious, uninhibited, adventure-seeking or controversial. Don't expect them to ask you to go parachuting, try a hot air balloon trip, or plan an exotic vacation filled with surprises. NGB's don't like to make waves. They're never the first out on the dance floor and usually don't swear in front of others.

What NGB's need to know is that most of us want some mystery in our relationships. We want the other person to help make the decisions about where to go and what to do. NGB's almost always let the other person pick the date, time and location (again, trying to please). Their tendency to please may cause others to see them as boring or dull. Most partners wish the NGB would take charge some of the time.

If you look at someone and say, "There's just no chemistry," what you're really saying is, "There's no sexual attraction." The truth of the matter is that when two naked people are under the sheets with the lights off, *looks matter much less than how loving and sensual you are.*

Remember:
It is better to be first with someone who is average, than last with someone who is drop-dead gorgeous!

TIPS FOR NGB's
Getting to the First Date and Beyond

1. Update your hairstyle. Consult an image specialist or tell your hairdresser that you want a "hot" or "spicy" hairstyle.

2. **Men:** Watch the movie "Dirty Rotten Scoundrels," in which Michael Caine teaches Steve Martin how to walk, dress, and act to woo women.

3. Dress to impress your dates or future prospects and then add just a little more sex appeal.

4. Take seminars designed to improve your self-confidence, assertiveness, and personal pizzazz.

5. Attend a Flirting Seminar or go out with a friend whose flirting skills are impressive and have him/her coach you while you practice. Try your local happy hour or a friendly atmosphere.

6. Always expect good service. Order what you really want on a date, and when it isn't just right, send it back. Don't be afraid to make small waves.

7. Never forgive someone who stood you up without a *good* explanation.

8. **Women:** Read the book *Secrets About Men Every Woman Should Know,* by Barbara DeAngelis, Ph.D. (P.S. Read it with your guy!)

9. Practice walking confidently. At first you may feel as if you look arrogant. Don't worry; that's something you'll never be.

10. Smile more on your dates, laugh, have a great time, and sometimes **do the unexpected.**

11. Avoid being too "available." Don't leave every Saturday night open just in case s/he calls. Make other plans if you are not invited somewhere by Wednesday, or Thursday at the latest. If you are too accessible to the opposite sex you may be labeled an NGB and/or be taken for granted.

An NGB analogy: When you come home to your pets, the dog jumps on you, pants, barks, drools and gets all excited. The cat, on the other hand, meows, rubs up against you and then disappears. Cats rarely wear out their welcome, but the dog gets pushed away. NGB's can appear too eager, like the puppy. NGB's need to avoid behavior that makes them seem a bit needy and smothering.

> *Try to be more like the mysterious cat*
> *who brushes up against you just so subtly*
> *and invitingly. . . then wanders away,*
> *returning every once in a while.*

I've coached men and women who have been the smotherer. They call a little too often, want to be with their dating partner every day, and call when they return home from a date, just to make sure their partner is okay. They also do too much to try to please by sending too many cards, sending flowers too often, etc. These behaviors put out their partner's flame. The "puppy's" feelings are authentic and s/he is *so into their emotions* of love and infatuation that they tend to go overboard. In the case of the smotherer, absence **does** make the heart grow fonder.

If you know that you have been guilty of smothering, don't plan to spend every Friday and Saturday with your love interest, even if you think you've met the person you've been waiting for all of your life. It's not easy but you can do it. "Meow!"

You deserve to

find,

give,

and receive love.

You have spent a lot of time

on your career;

now it's time to invest in your love life!

The "Loving Paycheck" is worth it.

**He liked people,
therefore people liked him.**

-- Mark Twain

**The most important thing a father can do
for his children is love their mother.**

-- Anonymous

Top Five Worst Dates

1. "He gave me a lecture when I didn't finish my food. Yes, I've heard about the 'starving children in Africa.' After dinner we went to a comedy club and he didn't laugh even once. I never went out with him again."

2. "On our first date we went out to dinner. She just about ordered everything on the menu and then wanted to know how much money I made per hour. That was enough for me. I never called her again."

3. "Friends thought we'd be great together. . . They told me he's a bit shy, and he had recently lost his wife to cancer. He showed up 30 minutes late without calling but handed me a wrapped present. To my surprise, he had stopped at Victoria Secret's for some lingerie. I chalked it up to lack of dating experience and explained that although it was beautiful, it made me feel he was only interested in one thing. I honestly believe he didn't know any better, but flowers would have made a nicer impression."

4. "First, she was 45 minutes late. Then, when we were done with dinner she disappeared into the bathroom for 30 minutes without an explanation. When I asked if everything was all right, she said, 'I just wanted to freshen up.' I started to wonder if she were bulimic, because I find it difficult to believe that a woman going to a non-busy restroom alone could possibly take that long. This happened twice more that evening. I couldn't handle it."

5. "His idea of a date was meeting at happy hour to get free appetizers and ordering only a diet coke. He knew everyone by name at every happy hour place and knew the menu of every establishment on any given day of the week."

Chapter Six

How to Make Every Man or Woman Want You

(Ten Secrets for Men)

For centuries, men have asked, "Why do some men seem to have a never-ending supply of women and others don't?"

Secret #1:   **It doesn't really matter what you look like, you can still become a "chick magnet!"**
You've seen it before. A blond bombshell walks by, and when you see who she's with, you ask, "How did *he* get *her*? He must be rich!" Usually these men figure they have nothing to lose and everything to gain by taking a risk.

Secret #2:   **Many beautiful women spend weekends alone because men ass-ume they:**
- are already taken.
- require too much care and maintenance.
- might reject them.

Heads turn when a gorgeous woman walks by. It's a fact of life. Men can be intimidated by the prospect of too much competition from other suitors. Men and women are reluctant to go after someone that they think is exceptional. Many people think that the possibility of being turned down by someone you've only dreamed about is not worth the risk. For this reason, some men prefer a woman who is pretty but not a knockout. The thought of competing and trying to measure up to other men makes them "play it safe."

Secret #3:   **Make a woman laugh and she will love you.**
Develop a more active sense of humor if you tend to be
too serious, or quiet and shy. Find two non-sexual
jokes to tell a woman; they can help lighten up any
situation. Practice the punch line until it feels natural.
That's what comedians do!

Borrow this joke for starters.
A guy walks into a bar and says to the bartender, " Hey,
do you mind if I tell an ethnic joke? It's Polish."
The bartender responds, "I guess I don't mind, but I'm
Polish, and so are those two ladies at the end of the bar.
Our bouncer is Polish and so is the owner. So, do you
still want to tell your ethnic joke?"
The guy quips, "Heck, No! Why would I want to have
to explain it five different times!"
Hint: Don't tell any "blonde" jokes unless you know
she won't be offended. 75% of women surveyed were
offended by gender jokes and blonde jokes, so don't
risk it, until you know her better. In fact the above
joke (and any good joke) can be told effectively
without using nationalities or race.

True or made up stories work well, too. My favorite
is the one where I went to an Espresso bar to get a cup
of Mocha and a Russian tea biscuit. After taking the
biscuit to my table, I realized that I did not order the
Mocha. When I turned around I saw this person sitting
down at my table who began to eat my treat! I rushed
over with my drink and said "Hey, you're eating my
food." I couldn't believe it when this person looked up
and said "So, do you have a receipt for it?" I walked
away dumbfounded and figured this person needed the
biscuit more than I did. A few minutes later the biscuit
thief left and I noticed a small shopping bag was still
under the table. Well, I couldn't help myself....I just

had to go and claim it. A few minutes later the biscuit-nabber returned looking frantically for the shopping bag. Imagine the look on this person's face when they saw it in my hands. The (now fatter) biscuit-nabber approached me in a huffy manner and said "You have my bag." To which I responded "So, do you have a receipt for it?" The Nabber squealed back, "Well, I'll just call the police and the manager," and then just disappeared. So, I just kept the bag.

Notice that not once did you know the sex, race, or nationality of this individual. It's simply not needed to make my point. I'm sure you're probably wondering what was in the bag? Baloney, just like the rest of the story. Sorry I couldn't help telling you this. Try it on your own, change the details, maybe it was a hot dog, muffin, etc. It makes people laugh every time. You'll have fun waiting to see how long it takes before your victim asks you what was in the bag.

Secret #4: **Don't wear beige from head to toe. Dress with style and original flair!**
Avoid wearing jeans and a t-shirt on your first date or when you're out looking for someone special. Find a smashing pair of dressy or casual slacks and wear a pressed cotton or cotton/polyester shirt, preferably without stripes (stripes are more at home at the office than on the dance floor). Women prefer men in silk shirts (make sure it's not skin tight), and sweaters in colorful variations. Wear something touchable!

Secret #5: **Make a woman feel special and she'll secretly be impressed.**
It's old fashioned, I know, but *do* open doors (unless she makes it known that she prefers you don't). Pay attention to little details. If she mentions that her favorite color is blue, or her favorite flower is a calla lily, write that down and surprise her with a small blue

gift or calla lilies. She may never remember telling
you and the effect will be magic.

Secret #6:   **It truly doesn't matter how much money you make,
whether or not you're overweight, walk with a limp,
or are going bald. Many wonderful women would
love to have you in their lives.**
If you don't believe this, go see the movie "Only the
Lonely" with John Candy. Take notes on his unique
date locations and how he's just himself. **The lesson:**
be an original! Carbon copies get thrown away. Take
time to read books on relationships. Great
relationships don't just happen, they're cultivated.

Secret #7:   **Confident men are irresistible!**
Exude an air of *confidence, not arrogance*. Fake it 'til
you make it. Keep your chest out and chin level!
Practice acting confidently and you will become more
confident.

Secret #8:   **Treat everyone with respect.**
For instance, be a generous tipper. Caution: Don't
overdo it. It's extremely embarrassing to women when
a man forgets to leave a tip or barely acknowledges the
server. It's equally in bad taste to lavishly leave too
large of a tip just to "impress" your date. *Remember:*
**your date is watching how you treat other people to
get an idea of how you'll treat them and their
friends.**

Secret #9:   **Don't be afraid to interrupt a conversation.**
Women feel more comfortable traveling in pairs or
groups. If you're interested, don't wait until two
women finish talking. **Politely interrupt. Always use
phrases like, "Excuse me" or "Pardon me" to get
their attention unless you've already established
smiling eye contact.** Find a fun and flattering way of

getting her attention and then ask for a dance, etc. If she's interested in you at all, she'll forgive your interruption, and actually like you more for doing it so politely.

Secret #10:   **It's a secret, unless you call the author at 216-521-LOVE (5683)!**

(Secrets for Women)

Secret #1

As much as you've been hurt and are skeptical of men the Number One Secret to having "Every Man" want you is to:

LOSE THE => "I HATE MEN RIGHT NOW !" ATTITUDE

Men can hear this attitude in your voices and see in your body language. When men sense this attitude, they will avoid you like the plague.

You may be secretly hoping the right man will come along and change your mind about men. You could be hoping that there is one more great one out there. He's unique, right? Guess Again. Some of the very men that you have been putting to the test, (passively asking them to make up for all the wrongs you've experienced with other men in your life) as well as men you've ignored are the "unique gems" you are looking for. Your current mate, if you have one, needs to experience the woman he first met, often enough to recognize you as irresistible.

If you have been hurt recently, I understand your anger and frustration. I too, have suffered from the "I hate men." syndrome. Give yourself some time to heal. Vent with other women. Remember that men will remember any angry statements you make about former relationships. One man I coached, heard an exasperated divorcee state : "I never want to get married again." Unfortunately, he believed her and gave up hopes of marrying her. The relationship ended when it did not need to. He misinterpreted her venting of emotions. Try to avoid this pitfall.

Secret #2: Take time out to dress sensuously without revealing too much. Refer to Image Chapter. More secrets can be found in The Companion Guide.

Ernie, A Nice Guy Period!!

Top Ten Male Fashion No-No's!
(According to women surveyed)

10. Men whose cheeks show when they bend over.

9. Wearing T-shirts that are too short and expose rolls of fat above the pants.

8. Wearing an undershirt that has a soiled, torn, or very worn, discolored-looking appearance. Wear new or v-necked undershirts. **Tip:** "Hot " men don't wear undershirts!

7. Unironed and unpressed clothes. Even wash-and-wear clothing needs touch-up pressing. (Take the easy way out: send them to a cleaner.)

6. Nerdy shoes or sandals.

5. Ties: (Try Jerry Garcia ties.)
   A. Tied too short over a large stomach.
   B. Knot is tied too large.
   C. Boring, one-color ties.
   D. Double knit or 100% polyester ties.
   E. With spots.
   F. Too ordinary (e.g. small polka dots or stripes).
   G. Knit ties (they look too much like socks).
   H. Skinny ties.
   I. Power ties (save them for the office).

4. Four hairs combed over a balding head. You're fooling no one! Women prefer a shaved head.

3. Long irregular finger and toe nails.

2. Buttons loose and hanging from clothing.

1. Hair parted down the middle.

I almost forgot to mention this and I can't believe that I even have to say this but,...you wouldn't believe the number of calls I get from women complaining that their dates have worn the same pair of shorts, the same sweater, or tie for five consecutive dates. It makes women think that you don't change your underwear too. A very big turn off!

Chapter Seven

Looking Irresistible!

Image and Fear of Rejection

Our image is an outward expression of our level of self-esteem. All human beings share the fear of rejection, which can affect self-esteem, confidence, and performance in daily life. How easy is it for you to confront someone who cuts in line, ask the boss for a much-deserved raise, or ask someone for a date?

Let's talk about the word "fear" and its effects on us emotionally as well as physiologically — even at a cellular level. When we experience fear, our bodies physically react, pumping adrenaline to produce the "fight or flight" response: a racing pulse, rising blood pressure, and dilated pupils. Our sense of awareness is heightened.

Before all of these responses were triggered in your body, your brain had to take in information, interpret the findings, and then come up with a diagnosis of the situation. Where did your brain get the interpretation? The fact is that fear is produced from experiences, our past programming, and "self talk." Once our senses have monitored the environment, pre-programmed thought patterns take over. In the movie "The Sound of Music," Julie Andrews gives an excellent technique for overcoming negative interpretations, or "feeling bad" (remember the song, "My Favorite Things"?). Self-help books also describe this kind of "good" thinking to us, so why don't we use such techniques to overcome it? The "it" to which I'm referring is negative past programming. Could it be that "it" is so simple that we don't believe "its" power? (Water is simple, too, but a flood can wash away everything in its path.)

To overcome negative self talk or programming see the section on Relating Skills in the *Companion Guide*, the challenging belief technique, and the Relating Section. Don't let fear keep you from realizing your best looks, optimizing your health, and capitalizing on your best assets, or, in short, from attracting the best relationship.

Appearance counts!

If you were the cover of a book, would anyone want to check out the inner contents?

Most men do not realize it, but from the beginning, women observe them and start evaluating how well they might fit into their life in a longer-term arrangement such as living together or marriage. If she cannot see these as possibilities, he's out. This is important, so let me repeat it. *If a woman checks you out and determines that you have too many qualities that would prevent her from wanting a "long-term lease," you're history!* This is not to say that men don't also qualify the women they are seeing, but in general, men tend to overlook the annoying things in the beginning of a relationship and use a test of time (for example, getting through twelve separate experiences of PMS). On the other hand, if a woman sees the potential of a toxic relationship when she first meets you, she might decide to end the relationship before the third date.

Men, now that you know that this happens, it would be an intelligent move to discover one of the "problems areas" most women analyze.

One of the first qualifiers is how a man dresses. Women look to see whether they could comfortably introduce you to their friends. The first thing a woman is likely to complain to me about is what a man wore on the first date. No matter how much fun he is, if a man is poorly dressed, he may not get a second chance. Some women will give men a couple more chances to redeem themselves, but usually no more than that.

Tips on hair: A friend and mentor, Robert Panté (author of *Dressing to Win*), says that people need to have just the right amount of sex, money, and career in their hairstyle. I agree. Sometimes people have too much sex in their hair. You know the look: too fluffy and flying everywhere. People who have too much of a career-only look to their hair can seem pretty boring. The look of money or prosperity comes from shiny, healthy well-trimmed ends and natural looking color. Men sometimes look more debonair and sophisticated with natural graying at the temples.

A note on baldness: Most women prefer a guy who's completely bald to one who wears a toupée, hairpiece, or wig. Nearly all women detest hair that is parted on the side, close to the ears, and then stretched over the top of the head. Whether it is swirled around or a few strands are pulled across, strongly consider getting the clean shaven look. Admit to your hair loss — it's much more refreshing to meet someone who can be comfortable with it. Try wearing a t-shirt that says, "Just another sexy bald guy."

More tips:

- Stay away from flannels, plaids, and clothes that make you look like a carbon copy. Note: grooming is more essential than colors.

- Invest in some light starch and an iron, or treat yourself to having the cleaners do your clothes. It is hard to fault a well-manicured man with good hygiene, who is dressed in a freshly pressed shirt.

- Use hand lotion. Make sure your hands are *clean!* (Who wants to touch hands dyed green from mowing the lawn?) Get a manicure, if you've never had one. Many men get hooked on the hand massage.

- Some men could really benefit from a facial, especially men prone to blackheads and those that work in dirty, dusty environments where particles get embedded into the skin. Guys, you'll love the TLC of the massage.

- I know we shouldn't have to say this, but some people still need to hear it: Don't forget the toothpaste, mouthwash, and deodorant.

**Men: Dress with pizzazz and you'll
increase your success with women.**

Essentials of a Gentleman's Wardrobe

Women complain: "Most men don't have a clue how to dress."
"He either shows up dressed like a country bumpkin (cheap plaid shirt
and unpleated, unironed pants) or dressed too conservatively (tiny
polka dotted ties, striped ties, plain shirt, and a three piece suit)."

Minimums (You are allowed to have more!)

1 Dark Up-to-Date Suit: For dressy events like weddings, holiday
parties, casual benefits, cocktail parties, or dinner at a special
restaurant. Even men who don't normally wear suits must have one. I
stress: make sure it's up-to-date! Don't date yourself; your suit
should be no more than three years old. Dress for where you are
going, not where you have been in life. (It's almost a new century.
Three-piece suits are out for now. If you must, wear the suit without
the vest.)

1 Sport Jacket: Wear it with jeans for a dressier look.

6 Ties: Avoid knitted ties that look like socks. Try to buy the best
quality tie your budget allows. Avoid solid and striped ties; women
prefer men in ties with lively patterns or more sophisticated designs.
    Your tie is your signature, much like a woman's jewelry. Try
three-dimensional designs that look like they are going somewhere.
Paisleys, florals, geometrics, and artistic designs fit the bill. When
you wear a tie that has your hair and/or eye color in the design or
background, it will give a message of trustworthiness. Black and red
ties project a message of power and presence but do not always create
approachability. The goal is to have universal appeal while attracting
the kind of women you would be interested in. A great tie can be a
conversation starter and ice breaker (let her be the first to speak). . .
especially if it includes teal and purple in combination with other
colors. As soon as a tie shows signs of wear and tear, toss it!

2 Pairs of Dressy Pants: 1 pair 100% wool and 1 pair cotton,
preferably with pleats.

2 Colorful Sweaters: Not just navy! The more touchable (read: great texture) the better. Sweater sales will go up and up when men realize how much more desirable and approachable they become to women when they wear "fantastic" sweaters. They are available in cool, thin cotton, or cotton/silk/wool combinations. Remember, the more colorful and touchable the better.

1 Pair Dress Shoes: Preferably loafers with a low vamp, so a woman can glimpse your "socks appeal." Resist buying ten pairs of black socks just because they're easier to match.

Socks: Coordinate and compliment your clothes. Socks should not slide down to your ankles, show hairy legs when you cross your legs, or have holes. Try patterned socks that say you are an original who pays attention to detail. Women love men with socks appeal.

Underwear: boxer shorts, bikinis, briefs: No holes or stains. Boxers are okay in fun colors and extra enticing in silk. Dare to wear colorful silky briefs; women like to touch them more.

1 Pair of Fresh/New Sneakers: Save the grungy ones to wear out with the guys or when working in the yard.

**As outward beauty disappears,
one must hope it goes in!**

-- Tennessee Williams

**The only service a friend can really
render is to keep up your courage by
holding up to you a mirror in which
you can see a noble image of yourself.**

-- George Bernard Shaw

Women Need to Spruce Up, TOO!

Men Complain:

- "I either find women with potential who need a tune up (makeup, more flattering clothing, accessories) or one who worries too much about her looks."

- "She wears so much makeup it actually makes her look older."

- "She spends so much time on hair, makeup and looking perfect that I'm afraid to touch her. If I mess it up she'd get upset. This kind of woman probably wouldn't make the best mother."

- "I wish she would wear just a bit more makeup and accent her eyes to make her more mysterious."

- "I don't feel she's really dolling herself up enough. I want her to make herself irresistible."

Glamour Shots₍®₎ has proven that you can take any woman: do her hair, makeup, and pose her in ritzy clothes and she can become visually "Hot!" On the other hand, if you saw magazine cover models before they do their hair and makeup, you'd probably not sense any "chemistry" with them either. Remember, men: any woman you meet can turn your hormones on if she treats herself well.

I've often taken my own clients and had them take a good look at themselves in the mirror. So many people do not really see their own beauty. Do not pass up wonderful women, based on looks alone. Take another look at her best features, and again at the whole. Maybe what you see at first glance is her hair, or a great shape, but what about the way she smiles, how her eyes light up when she sees you, the grace of her gestures?

**Kindness in women, not their beauteous looks,
Shall win my love.
-- *Shakespeare*
The Taming of the Shrew Act IV, Sc. ii, 1. 41**

Nadia Before

Nadia After

Nadia's before made men describe her as a stereotypical librairian or their aunt. After spending several thousand dollars on a dating service with little results, she traded her "ultra conservative look" for this sensual, up-to-date , and more alluring style.

Like Nadia, I've taken many clients shopping, and helped them develop a sense of personal style that speaks more of where they are going than where they've been. Often people feel guilty spending money on themselves to look good and never really give themselves permission to dress in a way that makes them feel irresistible inside and out. Nadia is enjoying her new look and left me this voice mail message :"I had men following me out of the auditorium, all vying for my attention! I'm loving it."   After a few changes, Presto! Three dates a week without the aid of the dating service.

(Better Eye Contact)

(Better Sweater)

Steve's "before" shows him in a pretty nondescript striped shirt, the type that does not make anyone look like an original. One of my mentors, Robert Panté, always said, "Carbon copies are cheap, they get thrown away, be an original!" The purple, creme, and gold textured sweater he is now wearing is much more tempting.

Susan Before

Susan After

This is my own "before," (13 years ago) AS you can see, I never ask anyone to try something I wouldn't be willing to do myself.

Take a few minutes and look in the mirror. What could you change to make yourself more irresistible? If you were the cover of a book, would anyone want to know what's inside? Choose your look with your life's goals in mind.

John-Before

John-After

John's "before" is okay, but just okay It doesn't make him look exceptional. So off to the hairdresser we went. He has hair most women only dream about. We chose new glasses, had the hairstylist teach him how to get rid of the middle part, and found wonderful clothes that helped him eliminate the "band roadie" look. He's very sexy, very single, and very available, as are Nadia and Steve.

Our thanks to Glamour Shots® 1-800-Glamour for the use of Nadia's and Susan's after.

Always dress to impress yourself and feel attractive.
But also remember that you aren't the only one affected by
your visual expression.

Single women disqualify themselves with men by dressing in non-visual, anti-sensual ways. Married women cause their husbands to lose interest in them by not paying attention to their appearance.

There are many ways to dress which should be chosen well, to emphasize not only what we want to communicate about ourselves, but also to indicate a target audience. Women and men can fall into any one of these four basic categories:

1. Dressing for women.
2. Dressing for men.
3. Dressing with universal appeal.
4. Dressing with no appeal.

Women's Image Styles Defined

1. Dressing for the Approval of Other Women

. . . is safe dressing. Everything is color coordinated; skirts are longer and blouses are buttoned up. Women always appreciate other women's accessories, hair styles, and clothes. We know when a woman is dressed to attract a man. Many single women make the mistake of dressing in a way that makes them look very unavailable (and/or very married).

If you are not regularly getting appreciative looks and compliments from men, take heed. (Of course, at times, you will not be interested in dressing for men, nor will it be appropriate.) Many women who have been widowed, divorced, or single for a long time make the mistake of dressing in clothes that are not conducive to attracting men.

Women in their 50's and 60's will need to lose the permed-all-over look and try a more updated hairstyle. Lose the gray even if you've earned it. More and more women age themselves by going natural when they have young attitudes and younger-looking skin. Try a hairdresser with a fabulous reputation and say you want to have the look of sex, money, and career in your hair.

Focus on your assets. If you have great legs, show them off.

Remember: Age is a number, youth is an attitude.

2. Dressing for Men
. . . Suggestive, alluring, and sensual!

Men do not appreciate ruffles, subtle fabric differences, and coordinated accessories like we do. They want to see your shape, even if it isn't perfect. They will focus more on your eyes, smile and other anatomy. They want us to wear suggestive clothing without showing it all.

- V-necked blouses, softer, more touchable hair, zippered clothing, buttons that start at your neck and end at your toes, asymmetrical skirts, form fitting clothes, tighter jeans.

- Brighter colors: red is number one! Wear black for sensuous hot evenings, or teal and purple in sexy styles for more approachability. Wear clothes that show you have a waist, a chest, and legs. Leave simple dresses and skirts that look like tents at home.

- Loosen up a bit. Wear brighter lipstick; red lets them know you're available.

- Watch your eyeglasses — they will tell on you too. Make sure you are wearing anti-reflective ultra thin lenses to avoid the coke bottle look. Treat you eyeglasses as if they were an important piece of jewelry. You wear them everyday, so spend some money on them and choose frames that say you are fun, alluring, and adventurous. Stay away from frames that make you look too conservative or intelligent--the big plastic coke bottle frames. Go for color and panache. Try a bi-colored metal, so that they go with all of your accessories. Buy two pair of eyeglasses. One that says you are unique and the other that says you mean business!

- Coloring hints: If you naturally have:
  Dark hair and light skin:
  wear the brightest red that you can find.
  Blond hair, light eyes, skin that burns:
  wear medium bright red or coral red.
  Blond hair, light eyes, skin that tans well:
  try a less bright red.
  Medium brown hair, skin that tans well, light eyes:
  wear a softer red.
  Medium brown hair, dark eyes:
  wear medium red.
  Redheads who tan:
  need bluer red lipstick and those that don't should wear brick reds.
  If you have Gold tones in your skin:
  avoid yellow/orange reds; try a blue-red.
  Note: Most women of Italian, Hispanic, African American, or Oriental descent can wear the brightest reds effectively.

- The Chanel suit look is appealing to men because of its simplicity and because it emphasizes shape. The flowing, romantic, long dress with a belted waist becomes male-friendly when it's unbuttoned to the knees or has a slit on the side.

- Shoes with designs on them, cut-outs on the side, and showing toe cleavage. Don't forget high heels.

- Dress to favor men's eyes when you are out looking for a man, out with your man, and in the bedroom.

3. Universal Appeal

. . . Means always dressing to please both sexes and almost any audience. Great for work, church/synagogue, going out with the girls, and at home. The flowing romantic belted dress becomes more appealing when it shows a little leg, is open at the neck, and is combined with high heels. When wearing flat shoes, accent the front of the foot or the heels. Try not to dress solely for comfort; keep it in mind, but err on the side of sensual. Hair is well groomed and healthy. Fingernails an average length. Basically take your clothes and add some spark, a creative flair, and express the innermost you.

4. No Appeal
Some of the symptoms: Dressing to just fit in. Wearing tent dresses, unless you are pregnant. Wearing fake eyelashes that are too long. Fingernails that look like weapons. Big baggy clothes that show no shape. Lifeless hair. Blue eye shadow on blue eyes. Not enough blush, or blush applied too heavily. Fingernails of varying length. No sense of color or wearing colors that make you disappear.

Irresistible Body Language

For Women:
- Men will notice you more when you sit up straight and proud. The higher you hike your leg when it's crossed the more available you will appear to a potential partner — even when wearing slacks. Arch your back slightly. Walk proudly with energy and wear a smile. Imagine that your head is attached to a string with a balloon and you float across the room (this is a great stress reliever, too).

- Make eye contact for at least three seconds with a smile, five seconds if you really like what you see, then look away. Be enthusiastic and interested in others.

- Dance with the first man who asks you, no matter what he's like. Other men are secretly watching and taking notes.

- Never laugh, make faces, or whisper to your friends immediately after a man who approaches you leaves your area; it will discourage other men from approaching you. When out with friends, always separate and plan lulls in your conversation so that a man can approach you without feeling like he's interrupting.

For Men:
- Take up space; it projects an air of confidence. Lean back a bit in your chair while your eyes are cruising the horizon for a potential

partner. Walk with energy, as if you are very tall. Picture yourself as confident, and project that image!

- Do not be apologetic for who you are and what you look like. Hold your head level, shoulders back. Women find this combination irresistible.

For Both Sexes:
- **Imagine that you have attached a gold chain to your sternum (CPR rescuers know where that is.). Now imagine pulling straight up on that gold chain. Notice your chest rise and your rib cage no longer sits on your hips. You can breathe easier and you'll feel more energized.**

Love is the finest cosmetic in the world.

-- Frances Brooke

Cheerfulness and contentment are great beautifiers and famous preservers of good looks.

-- Charles Dickens

Top Ten Female Fashion No-No's
(According to Most Men)

10. Heavy women who wear stretch pants with stirrups that don't cover up their ass-ets! Learn to create visual balance. Try the book *Flatter your Figure*, whether you are a size 2 or 22.

9. Too much makeup or not enough. Heavy blue eye shadow on blue eyes is out (it's better to wear a soft brown or charcoal.)

8. Wearing large bulky clothes that cover up your shape. Call 216-521-IMAGE (4624) to order *Flatter Your Figure.*

7. Men don't mind runners in your stockings as much as you do. However, men prefer not to see runners in black stockings.

6. Too much perfume!

5. Hair that men are afraid to touch (hair with too much hairspray or fixed so perfectly that they are afraid it would upset you if they messed it up).

4. Men actually like to see panty lines in your clothes. (X marks the spot!) Men would prefer your clothes worn more snugly than loosely.

3. Clothes that disguise or hide your shape. Men prefer simple color schemes and designs that lend to their imagination; wrap dresses and skirts, straight skirts, v-necks or scoop necks are great! Front zippered dresses, button down dresses, off the shoulder, and asymmetrical designs work well, too.

2. Women who wear dresses or suits with running shoes and socks.

1. Least favorite hair style: Hair that is too round, short and curly (a short, very curly perm). One man said it reminded him too much of pubic hair.

Top Ten Flirting Tips

1. Effective flirting is simply a way to let someone know that you noticed them and want to get to know them.

2. The most effective flirting always include a smile and eye contact.

3. At least 3 attempts at verbal or non-verbal contact are necessary to establish sincerity. **This is the Repeated Contact Rule.**

4. If a woman brushes up against you, watch for eye contact as confirmation that she is interested in your making the next move.

5. Use this elegant line when waiting in line, at a wedding, in an elevator, etc.: "Pardon me, it's a shame that no one is here to properly introduce us. Do you mind if I do the honors?"

6. Compliment people and follow up with an open-ended question that requires more than a yes or no answer, e.g. "Great hair style. Who is your hairstylist?"

7. If you are nervous, remember that it's *normal* to feel that way. Tell yourself, "I feel like I have butterflies in my stomach. I must *really* want to meet this person." Then go for it!

8. When you enter a room full of strangers, look across the crowd as if you see someone you know, then wave. Believe it or not, you'll feel more at home. Sounds crazy, but it works! (You'll get noticed and may find yourself smiling and more at ease.)

9. Remember the feeling that someone is staring at you? When you turned around, they *were* looking at you. Consider this feeling a transfer of energy and mentally send good energy back.

10. Body language, body language! Keep your chin level, shoulders back, stand up straight, and walk with confidence.

Chapter Eight

Flirt, Flirt, Flirting!
How to Flirt and Not Look Like You are in Heat!

**I am Tarzan of the Apes. I want you.
I am yours. You are mine.**

*-- Edgar Rice Burroughs
Tarzan of the Apes* (1914), ch. 18

When I tell people that I teach flirting techniques, they automatically assume that I was always a flirt. Not so! I began to research flirting because I was shy and needed to learn how to flirt *successfully*. Like so many people, I had to learn to overcome the fear of rejection.

Somehow flirting has acquired a negative connotation. Successful flirting isn't what it used to be. **Today, men need to be more subtle.** Use fewer "lines" and more sincerity. **Women need to be more obvious when flirting** (that's so the guys can *really* tell when we're interested). I teach people how to flirt and not look like they are in heat, how to have fun, overcome shyness, and send the word "rejection" back to the dark ages. Flirting is really just another form of communication which lets someone else know that you've noticed them. Flirting changes our moods and makes us more playful.

Flirting (my new definition):
**A playful form of communication which
acknowledges another human being and
expresses interest such that the opposite party can
respond verbally or non-verbally to indicate
a desire to meet or avoid open rejection.**

If you're interested in overcoming rejection and learning what the opposite sex really wants, open your mind, and try some of the flirting tips in the following pages.

The human heart, at what ever age, opens to the heart that opens in return.

-- Maria Edgeworth

Flirting Fundamentals

The meaning of communication is the response you get to the message you send. Flirting is just that: another means of communication (and a fun one, if you've practiced). The subtle art of flirting is one of the most enjoyable ways to meet others.

Flirting: A form of communication which allows you to acknowledge someone in a positive way thereby increasing rapport and interest.

-- Susan Bradley

No other form of communication allows you to:
1. See someone you're interested in, then,
2. Communicate your interest in a flattering way,
3. Prevent open rejection and,
4. Create an opportunity to meet someone previously beyond your grasp.

Flirting can brighten your day and make you smile, or it can make your heart thump. But don't let it scare you. Flirting just might open up a new realm of opportunities for meeting quality people. On the whole, flirting is a relatively non-threatening way to see if another person is interested in getting to know you further. Gaining flirting expertise paves the way to a new level of comfort and allows you to meet new people with ease. Those who feel they are above flirting, or who label it as a game, will miss out simply because they don't understand it.

One of the most frequently asked questions is, "When is flirting perceived as a come-on?" There are all types of flirting, verbal and non-verbal. Flirting can be anything from smiling and telling a grandmotherly type person how gorgeous she is, to overtly soliciting a response by blowing kisses to a man or woman and licking your lips (which is an obvious come-on). The next question is usually, "How do I know when to use 'open' versus 'subtle' flirting?" The answer varies with the situation. You must begin by trusting your intuition in interpreting non-verbal body language.

Flirting is part body language
and part innuendo.

Example 1: You're sitting in an expensive restaurant when you notice an attractive person glancing your way. To see if that person is interested, glance back with a smile on your face. If this person smiles back, you can be fairly sure s/he's interested. It isn't appropriate to wave. However, if you're at a crowded, jovial social affair, such as happy hour in a singles hangout, waving would be fine.

Example 2: You're on a semi-crowded elevator during business hours and notice someone you would like to meet. Compliment this person on something they're wearing. You'll be able to tell right away if: a. they are available, and b. you can continue conversation. *Warning!* Commenting on a woman's anatomy, such as, "Great legs!" is a NO-NO! While it's certainly a compliment, it decreases the chances of actually continuing conversation. She may not know what to say, and will feel uncomfortable. Such comments could also be considered sexual harassment and could end your job. Use discretion!

All flirting should begin and end with a smile. Below are some tried and true flirting techniques.

1. Winking.

2. Taking your glasses partially off to get a better look.

3. Second glances over your shoulder.

4. Say, "I wish there was someone here to introduce us, do you mind if I do the honors?" (This technique works better if you've already had some non-verbal communication, as listed in techniques 1 - 3, and the person seems receptive.)

5. Fluffing or arranging your hair (ladies only).

6. Raising one eyebrow while glancing toward someone.

7. Most women hate runners in their stockings but when it comes to flirting, they can be your best friend. The following scenario will definitely arouse interest and create an interesting dilemma. The next time you notice that you have a run in your hose, **try the "pantyhose runner line."** Point to your runner and say, "Do you know where runners come from? Did you ever wonder where they go? Guess how long my runner is."
If you want to take it a step further, say, "Would you mind putting your finger here?" Place his finger at the end of the runner and say, "Yes, there. Now, are you prepared to be the guardian angel of my runner? Do you promise to prevent this runner from getting any larger? Hey, hey, hey! Don't let go, unless you're willing to take full responsibility for this runner." Oh, and ladies, while he's touching your runner (hopefully in a decent spot) carry on a perfectly normal conversation. Pretend that he isn't doing anything out of the ordinary. This is an experience he'll never forget, and neither will you.

Fabulous *Flirting* Tips

1. Always, always *make eye contact!* Why? It lets them know you are interested!

2. **Remember his/her name!** This will set you apart from the rest of the crowd.

3. Start a conversation with a witty comment. For example, try this at a health club: "Your legs must be tired. . . they've been running through my mind *all night!"* Be creative; try something new, not a tired line.

4. **Don't talk too much. Ask questions instead!** Let the other person tell you how great they are, which will make them feel more comfortable about giving you their phone number.

5. Use body language. . . *Blow a kiss!*

6. Be willing to risk, be creative, and *never* take it personally if they are not interested! Never feel rejected. Hey, it might be their loss anyway!

7. How about the "*CLASSIC WINK*"? It's not used as often as it should be.

8. HAPPY HOUR: If someone offers to buy you a drink, accept it if you like. Remember, however, that you do not have to buy one in return. Too often people feel obligated to reciprocate. Do say "thanks" with a toast of the glass or *in person!*

9. When at a gathering, offer your seat to a person who appears to be unaccompanied. Stay near that area and *start talking to them.*

10. **Ask a clever question,** such as : "Would you mind if I flirted with you?" It works! You'll know if s/he is interested in you right away. (If they respond, "Well, I wouldn't mind, but my

girlfriend/husband might," don't feel rejected. Just move on to someone else.)

11. SMILE, SMILE, SMILE! You're interested, right?

12. **Be honest**. If there is no chemistry or real interest, don't give out your number!

13. Give them the all-over "look-over"! If you like what you see, let them know with a smile or a wink. Walk over and say hello. Offer to shake their hand.

14. Guys: try the gentle kiss on the hand. If it's spontaneous and not too affected, it gets me every time. . . makes me feel warm all over! (No tongues please.)

15. **Compliment them!** Tell them how beautiful, original, handsome, intelligent, creative, special, sincere, helpful, colorful, genuine, etc., you think they are. Caution: Be sincere, and don't pile it on.

16. Remember the "CLASSY WHISTLE"? Not the brash wolf whistle heard on the street, it's a low, sexy version that makes people smile and feel great!

17. Ask to borrow something: a pen, a piece of paper, or anything else. This will give you more time to start conversation.

18. Try the infamous *bump into them by accident;* then say, "OOPS, I'm sorry!" The subtle sleeve brush works well, too.

19. LICK or "wet" YOUR EYEBROWS!

20. *Remember, just have fun no matter what. Life is too short not to!*

21. Touch the other person lightly and briefly on the arm while making eye contact. Be subtle; make it seem as if you were emphasizing a point in conversation.

22. Ask, "What are you passionate about?" or share some of your own passions.

23. Be honest about yourself. If you're nervous, say so. Honesty can be charming.

24. Humorously play act a romantic scene from a movie or play. You never know where your thespian skills could lead.

25. *Pay attention!* Really *listen* to what they say and how they act. These clues will help you determine whether or not you want to continue getting to know them.

P.S. Guys, if a woman is the slightest bit interested in you, she'll forgive you if you seem a bit nervous or end up tongue-tied.

Keep your marriage/relationship alive. . .
Flirt with each other often!

A good line is hard to resist.

--Mae West

Top Ten Worst Lines

1. Trust me.

2. Do you come here often?

3. What's your sign?

4. Are you the modern kind of woman who doesn't wear underwear?

5. Hey, baby ! Wanna screw?

6. Your place or mine?

7. I would like to go to bed with you.

8. If I told you that you had a beautiful body, would you hold it against me?

9. So what part of me do you find most arousing? Why are you looking at me like that? I don't want to have sex with you. I just want to sleep with you.

10. Are those yours or have they been surgically enhanced?

An Extra Helping of Worst Lines

We've all heard the worst ones before, the list is endless. Here's a few more to avoid.

1. He says: "Is that a mirror in your pocket?" She says: "Why?" He says: "Because I can see myself in your pants."

2. He licks his finger and touches your shoulder, then says, "Lets get these wet things off."

3. He walks up to you and says with a touch of surprise: "Do you know that you have the best body of any woman in this bar? What a great smile, too." (Some men practice this one until they have all of the body language down pat. They can be convincing but deadly.)

4. "What big hooters you have!"

5. "Can I take you home?"

6. "You turn me on."

7. "Lets have a one night stand."

8. "So, are you a woman's libber?" (No sexist comments, please.)

9. "What's happening?"

10. "Haven't I met you somewhere before?" (Even if you have, avoid this tired line. Try to be more specific: e.g., "You look familiar. Do you go to Mentor Headlands Beach? I just thought I might have seen you there.")

11. "Can I buy you a drink?" (Not everyone drinks alcohol, so offer to buy an appetizer or dessert.)

12. "Hey, do you come here often?" (Never use this as an opening line. Later in conversation, however, you could more safely ask if the woman you are speaking with is familiar with the menu, or if she has been to other events at the same location.)

Also Eliminate:
- Lines that make any reference to sex.
- Any line that begins, "Hey, baby. . . (chick, honey, or sweetheart.)"

Top Twelve Best Lines:

1. "You look wonderful tonight."

2. "You make me melt." (Better for women and couples to use.)

3. "If you aren't attached, I would love to go out with you." (Even if s/he is attached at this time, this line leaves room for future possibilities if they become unattached.)

4. "As attractive/handsome as you are, I bet you've heard every line in the book. . . So one more won't kill you."

5. Flirter (reaches out and grabs her arm): "You can't leave yet." Flirtee: "Why not?" Flirter: "Because I'm celebrating my birthday." Flirtee: "Oh, when's your birthday?" Flirter: "Next year, but I'm celebrating now anyway."

6. "I am so sorry that I missed your birthday. May I buy you a drink?" (Again, I recommend asking if you can buy a dessert or appetizer instead of a drink; it's just a bit more savvy.)

7. "You look very elegant and sophisticated."

8. "I hope you are just as beautiful inside as you are outside."

9. "If eyes are truly the mirrors of our souls, then my soul would love to meet yours."

10. "As soon as I noticed you, I knew that I'd have to find some reason for us to talk."

11. "So who do you look like most, your mother or your father?

12. "Excuse me, what is your name? I just had to know who I was dreaming about.

Be creative, humorous, and authentic with your initial approaches, then use conversation extenders to get you past the initial discomfort of the 5-10 second silence that occurs once you have used an introductory line.

Flirting Safaris™

Because it's a jungle out there and since flirting comes in many varieties, go on a Flirting Safari™ and observe human mating patterns. If you are super shy, get a modem for your computer and try out the romance connection chat lines on the Internet or America-On-Line and practice flirting in cyberspace. It's easier to flirt when you aren't face to face. I warn you, though: you will see both good and bad examples of flirting.

When I researched this subject, I took my students to a popular lounge during happy hour. We practiced attracting the opposite sex and using subliminal flirting skills. Go on your own Safari. Try some of the things I noticed others doing, such as:

The School Teacher: He had confiscated a small plastic football player from one of his students and used it for flirting. Obviously or sneakily (depending on his intended victim), he dropped it into women's drinks. I saw this ploy work many times. It gave him a very good excuse to buy her a drink and tested her to see if she was a good sport.

Sometimes, he would pretend surprise when she discovered the "little guy" in her drink, and he'd say "How did that get there? Can I buy you another drink?" Other times, he would confess and ask for forgiveness. Try this technique with plastic Smurfs or dinosaurs, too. (Women should try this one too! Guys are more likely to think it's funny and they'll be flattered when you buy them a drink.)

Made in Heaven (a much safer flirting technique that creates intrigue): A woman grasped a man's jacket, sweater, etc. She looked inside at the label, and said, "I just wanted to see if you were made in heaven" (smile, smile). If a man wants to try this with a woman, he should use her overcoat or be with someone he knows well. It could seem too threatening to a woman to have a man grasp her clothes, as it would be violating personal space rules.

So, Do You Want Me?: Someone I've known for a long time uses this surprising line with men who stare at her. She smiles and says in a soft voice, "So. . . do you . . . want me?" This question had different effects on different men, either producing confusion in the male, who didn't know what to say, or it broke the ice and made them both laugh. (This is definitely an Advanced Flirting Technique; try the Fabulous Flirting Tips first!)

Avoid stumbling and fumbling. Practice flirting at home while looking in the mirror, so that you don't stumble on the words. Pay attention to your body language and smile. Tilt your head at an angle to give the opposite sex a cue that you are flirting.
Remember, flirting is a harmless way to meet people. Do it for fun and flattery, and you'll be rewarded. If someone doesn't respond, don't take it personally. It's a lot easier to accept the subliminal, subtle clues flirting provides if someone is just not interested at the time.

If you and your friends would like to arrange a Flirting Safari™, and learn other flirting techniques: call (216) 521-LOVE (5683)

ZING! I met this woman who was so good at flirting, that when she slowly lifted her eyelids to look at me through the corners of her eyes, it was as if she had invited me to share her life with her.
Todd, Flirting Safari Attendee

ZING! I felt flushed all over when Colin smiled at me and held my eyes at attention for a few seconds longer than normal.

Mary, Flirting Safari Attendee

Flirting with Grrr-eatness For Men

- "I know this guy who lies to women about his age. . . he tells fibs about what he does for a living. He's 50 and he's always out with women in their 20's. . . lots of them! He's always bragging about how he does it. He's short, well-dressed, okay-looking but not overly handsome. What's he got that I don't?"

- "Randy is only 5'2", stocky, wealthy, obnoxious and into playing all the time. You should see the babes he's out with. He flashes cash. Is that what I need to do to get women?"

- "Jason is absolutely HUGE! He makes John Candy look tiny. Women follow him around like he's the president."

- "I'm bald, ugly, and have an average income, and women love me!"

Four different men. . . four different lives, but all have something in common: success with women!

Sure, you could flash some cash and lie to women just to get laid. But how long would it take before you run out of cash, begin to forget who you really are, and start believing that all women want is your wallet? You may think it doesn't hurt to lie about your age; after all, women do it all the time, don't they? Remember that the minute you lie to someone, you give them permission to deceive you, too.

Learn to **Flirt with Grrr-eatness** without using lies. Become GRRR-EAT! In our examples above, the first two men used superficial means to get involved with women. The last two used their assets; in fact, *they created their own assets.* These last two men know some secrets that y'all don't.

It's not how much money you have, or looks, or power, it's presence (not presents, PRESENCE). These men are conscious of the dynamics of personality. They learned how to be charismatic. Yes, I said, "learned." You can learn, too.

Lesson #1 : LOVE all women, appreciate them, smile at them, joke with them, and compliment them, no matter what size, shape, color, or age. Find something you like or appreciate about every woman you meet.

Lesson #2: Learn how to come from the HEART, not the hormones, with feeling and energy. Use your emotions! How do you do it? The minute a woman feels the connection of your emotional energy, you become a potential relationship partner. When a woman feels connected to you, she will overlook a multitude of flaws. In order to get to the point of connecting, you must be willing to give up what you already know about the rules of flirting.

Lesson #3: BE WILLING to be outrageous! Be funny! Be witty! and never, NEVER, NEVER EVER give up! You can learn to be outgoing.

Lesson #4: LEARN how to say one very important word in overcoming feelings of rejection: N-E-X-T! Then, move on. You don't have time to dwell on someone who doesn't want you. Find the woman who's wondering why you haven't approached her, talked to her on the elevator, or noticed that she's very interested in you.

Lesson #5: Learn and practice the Top 10 SEDUCTION Strategies. She wants you to use them but you must be willing. (See Directory of Love Advice at the end of the book.)

Lesson #6: LISTEN to women in a way that lets them know you heard them. Don't interrupt! Be an active listener: rephrase what you have just heard. For example: Jan: "You are so obnoxious. Do you know how many women are turned off by the way you act?" Bob: "So, you're saying that because I act a certain way, I turn women off?" Jan: "Yes, that's it." Bob: "Okay, then what should I do to improve my chances with a woman like you?" Jan: "Well, talk to me as if I have some brains." Bob: "I guess that means I have to give up my 'blonde' jokes, and not act surprised when I find out you are a neurosurgeon, right?" Jan: "You got it!"

Lesson #7: Notice BODY LANGUAGE that says she's *single* and *available* and interested in *you*: smiles, glances, fidgeting with her hair or clothes, nervous looks, or brushing up against you as she walks to the rest room. She may touch you lightly when making a point in conversation or commenting out of the blue. **Pay attention to signals you may have missed.**

Lesson #8: ACT on the subtle signals you receive. Introduce yourself, or get a friend to go up to her and say: "Excuse me what is your name? Judy? Judy, I'd like you to meet Joe. He's a very good friend of mine and I just wanted him to be introduced to you." Many women are disappointed because men don't recognize their "flirting signals." Begin noticing and take action!

Lesson #9: Be IRRESISTIBLE! An overwhelming percentage of women find men more irresistible in a suit and tie. Even if you don't wear suits for business, get some for play. Forget polyester suits and striped or tiny polka dot ties. *Dress to impress.* Wear colors that attract women: purple, red, teal, turquoise. On super-casual occasions wear a GRRR-EAT! t-shirt. (I didn't say crude; I said GRRR-EAT! For example, if you are very tall, have a shirt made that says, "Yes, the view is better up here!" If you are short: "Short men have BIG ♥'s." Or: "Wife Wanted. . . for moonlit nights, candle lit dinners, long walks on the beach, and more. Inquire here 4 info.")

Lesson #10: GIVE UP whining and moaning about your life and women. Live the moment! Learn to live outside your comfort zone long enough to produce results. RISK it to get it. Go for what you want. Keep going. . . and when you think you've tried it all, try something else.

Flirting with Grrr-eatness For Women

Women are so much more subtle about flirting clues so men need to pay attention. Ladies, men are not used to women flirting with them. A vast majority of men said they would just love it if a woman would initiate conversation or at least express interest in checking him out.

Lesson #1: Repeated contact: give at least three separate verbal or non-verbal clues. Why? The first time he'll look around and make sure it's really him that you are flirting with. The second time, he knows you're flirting with him and he'll get flushed and pleased. (At this point he'll probably walk by you and at least smile — he's checking you out a
little more.) The third time, you can express interest by introducing yourself, commenting on his tie, or waving from across the room. Now he knows you are open to meeting and it will be a cinch.

Lesson #2: Whisper. . . it always gets their attention! Ask if you can tell him a secret, then whisper in his ear, "I just love your tie. Can I buy it from you when you are done with it?"

Lesson #3: Don't sit with other women. Men don't want you to reject them in front of an audience. If you go out with a friend, separate every so often or take a breather from talking. Men do not want to risk your disapproval by interrupting you. (You have already missed out on a lot of quality polite men who didn't want to interrupt.)

Lesson #4: Treat men gently. If someone you are not interested in approaches you and flirts, *be nice*. All of the other men are watching to see what you do. If you laugh after he leaves or show obvious disapproval, you reduce the chances of anyone else approaching you. Try shaking his hand and saying something like: "It was so nice of you to approach me. What's your name? Jim? Jim, I know how hard it is to meet people. I might have a girlfriend who would be interested in you."

Lesson #5: IF he acts like a JERK! Be polite but firm. Hand him a copy of the men's version of "Flirting With Grrr-eatness" and ask him to go practice on someone else. Firmly state that "lines" with sexual overtones are not only *not* attractive to you but to most other women in the world. If all else fails, give men who need a flirting tune-up this phone number and I'll take care of them for you (216-521-LOVE).

Lesson #6: Use the buddy system. Walk through a group of men and have someone watch to see who's checking you out.

Lesson #7: Become more irresistible! Show a little leg, wear higher heels. The redder your lipstick the more available and noticeable you will be. Arch your back a little as you sit up tall and cross your legs high. Wear earrings that are interesting enough to elicit comments.

Lesson #8: Look over your shoulder. . . and smile at him. This asymmetrical position is always a signal you are interested.

Lesson #9: Give him a look all over from head to toe, nod with approval, and then flash him your most winning smile.

Lesson #10: Remember that flirting is a way of connecting from the heart and acknowledging someone. Be generous! **Have fun NOW!**

**Pretend you've known someone all of your life—
before you talk to or even approach them. It'll trick
your brain into a calmer and more positive state of mind.**

— Susan Bradley

Flirting, Part B
What to say after "hello"or any other ice breaker

There may be several uncomfortable silences in the beginning of a conversation with a stranger. When they occur, either use the opportunity to escape and come back later, or wait them out and use the time to think of something else to talk about. Lulls in conversation are to be expected. Someone will usually say something before a ten second pause is over.

Count ten seconds out now: one thousand one, one thousand two, one thousand three, one thousand four, one thousand five, one thousand six, one thousand seven, one thousand eight, one thousand nine, one thousand ten. Whew! In a conversation, when most people have reached "one thousand five," they begin to feel a little uncomfortable, and may feel internal pressure to come up with something witty to say. Relax, take a deep breath, and push through it. This will give you an edge.

Use the time to adjust your body language and think of a question related to current events, give another compliment, or ask for help ("Where should I go to eat?" Or, "Are there any new restaurants around here?"). Ask for directions, and while they; or you are writing them down you could playfully say, "Don't forget to write your number there too, in case I get lost." If the individual looks a bit surprised or uncomfortable, smile and say "Just kidding, but I wouldn't mind getting to know you later." Remember that if someone asked you for help, you'd naturally want to give it — so don't be afraid to ask others.

Tip: Even if you don't work somewhere that requires business cards, make up your own to hand out. Use a post office box for an address if you really want to play it safe. Business cards make you look more established, and are much easier to find (and keep in good condition) than a scrap of paper or a napkin. Personalize your card with color, favorite sayings, logos of hobbies, etc.

Conversation Starters and Extenders: Repeated contact lets the object of your attention realize that you aren't just playing with them. *It will definitely give the message that you are interested.* Keep the conversation going with light questions about universals, or "safe" topics that everyone can relate to, such as pets, vacations, work, and family. For example, "I'm planning a vacation. Have you ever taken a cruise? Have you been to Europe? What's your favorite vacation destination? Do you know a great travel agent?" If the person responds, "No, I haven't taken a vacation in years," or, "I can't afford a vacation right now," say, "That's a shame. Where would you go if you could?" You could also ask, "Why do you work so hard?

Another good conversation starter is to sigh and murmur, "I need a vacation; how about you?" Follow the generic comment with a flirtatious comment like, "I'd invite you to come along but I don't know you well enough. Do you travel well? You don't snore do you?" Or ask people if they have pets, how many, what kind, and do they do any neat tricks? Pet owners will talk for ages about their animals.

Try to keep the conversation light. Avoid heavy discussions about religion, politics, or anything on which you might disagree and lose rapport.

If you are sitting in a restaurant near someone you want to meet, lean over to their table, establish eye contact, smile, and say, "I can't decide; what's good on this menu?" Following the rule of repeated contact, ask another question: "I know, why don't I have you order for me and it will be a surprise!"

Don't let shyness get in your way. When you are out, ask where the nearest rest room is. If s/he is interested, s/he'll usually help you. Once again, use the rule of repeated contact. After you go and come back, thank the person, then use a conversation starter, like, "I noticed you from across the room. You've got a great smile. Do you have to practice to be that cheerful?"

If you've tried these techniques and find yourself striking out, you may be choosing people who are not compatible or are already taken. Thomas Watson, Sr., founder of IBM, said, "If you want to increase your success rate, double your failure rate." If you know ahead of time that some people will be interested in you and others won't, then you won't take it so personally when they don't feel like talking, are having a bad day, aren't available, speak another language, think you remind them too much of their ex, etc. Count on the fact that there will always be some people who will wonder why you are talking to them, ignore you, or say they're not interested. (Remember that one little word,

NEXT!) Move on. There are so many more people to meet, and at least you are getting good practice.

It is possible to lose your shyness, once you realize that people aren't going to bite your head off for initiating conversation.

Remember the repeated contact rule:

Let someone know you are interested

with three separate contacts

(verbal or non verbal).

One isolated comment made while walking by

someone does not create enough interest.

Top Ten Best Places to Meet the Opposite Sex

1. Seminars, adult education classes, or anywhere people are engaged in learning: If they're into learning, there's hope for a relationship.

2. Supermarkets: Look in their cart, then ask if a particular brand of whatever they are buying is really good or not. Make sure you initiate contact again and try to get in the same checkout line.

3. Laundromats: You're usually there long enough to check each other out. Ask a question about how the machines run. Check out their laundry — (Hey! At least they do their laundry.)

4. Bookstores with a coffee shop or espresso bar: Some have regular singles discussions. Carrying a book under your arm with the title visible makes it easier for someone to comment on it and start a conversation. If you are interested, smile, smile, smile.

5. Volunteer to work booths for charities: You'll find yourself in good company, benefit others, and talking to a lot of people.

6. Libraries, especially the periodical section: You don't need to be as quiet there. There's a lot of turnover and you can make sure you just happen to be checking out a magazine or newspaper right where Mr. or Ms. Potential is. (Now you know they can read.)

7. Waiting in lines for tickets (especially for concerts): You know you already have something in common (the concert).

8. Airports and airplanes: People generally have time to spare for small talk. You can meet someone from your own city on flights that leave and return from your hometown. Always try to sit by someone interesting, even if that means changing your seat.

9. Men's clothing stores and sporting good stores/women's clothing stores at sale time: Get a part time job there and you'll meet lots of people.

10. Art festivals, car exhibitions, art gallery openings, auctions, ski shows, hiking clubs, golfing : You both will have something in common and something interesting to talk about!

Top Ten Male Catches

1. Men who love being fathers and want to spend time with their children.

2. Men who participate in the "Big Brother" program.

3. Men who are part "NBG" (Nice Guy But. . .) They are usually more open to personal growth and development and don't already "know everything.

4. Men who have had a good relationship with their mothers and appreciate them.

5. Men who volunteer for charitable causes.

6. Men who know how to cook and like it.

7. Men who belong to service organizations, i.e. Rotary, Kiwanis, etc...

8. Men who aren't afraid to show their feelings openly.

9. Men who know the value of being romantic.

10. Men who are sometimes willing to wear the shirts and ties their women choose for them.

Chapter Nine

Dating Services and
Personal AD-ventures:
How to Make Them Work for You!

Finding someone special with whom to develop a successful relationship is up to you. The bar scene is being replaced by better alternatives, ranging from social clubs, church/synagogue groups, sports clubs, singles' events at book stores, and more. Matchmakers, video dating services (such as Great Expectations),and interactive computer dating services are flourishing. Personal AD-ventures (as I call them) have their role in this scene, too.

Intelligent people realize that their soulmate is not going to magically land in their back yard in a parachute and announce their arrival. Although at first it may seem "un-natural" to meet people via these services, try it. You have nothing to lose and everything to gain. *Tips:* **Play it safe. Be cautious regardless of the way you choose to meet new people**.

- Never give out your home address.

- Only use your first name.

- Get your own phone line if you live with your parents or an opposite-sex roommate.

- Spend the extra $10 per month (approximately) to gain the extra security of a voice mail number that is not connected to your home phone. Give out your home number only after they've passed your initial requirements.

- If you don't have one, get an answering machine. It boggles my mind that it's almost a new century and some single people don't have an answering machine that lets others leave messages when they are not at home.

The chart on the next page will help you compare the alternatives.

Type	Cost	Benefits	Pitfalls
Personal Ads	$	Inexpensive; available everywhere; reaches a wide variety of people; you can change your ad often. The more specific you are, the better your chances of meeting someone you'll hit it off with.	You'll spend a lot of time weeding through unqualified responses, having many phone conversations and meeting for "coffee." You'll meet people who do not fit their ads. To get the best results answer many ads.
Social Clubs	$-$$	Have fun while meeting others.	If you are shy, it could take you longer to meet others.
Dining Clubs	$-$$	Dinner conversation can be a wonderful way to meet someone.	Limited to the number of people attending.
Singles Dances	$	Great, if you like to dance or want to learn.	Limited to the number of people attending. The quality may disappoint you.
Match-makers	$$$	Someone else does the work; the more expensive the fee, the more selective the organization can be.	You may only meet ten people per year. You have limited control on who you'll meet.
Video Dating	$$$	Fairly thorough screening done in person; you make the selections or are guided; limitless choices; new members join daily; the best services have events and personal advisors; members are more serious about wanting a relationship	Beware of the inexpensive version of these services as they may not be able to provide quality members or quantity, and they may only cover a small geographic area. If you don't wear colors and styles that enhance your appearance, you may be passed over. Tip: Be reasonable. If you are 30 lbs. or more overweight, don't live in a glass house.

How to Get Irresistible Results
From Personal Ads

1. Use personal ads that include a voice mail message service.

2. Include a good photograph (not one that resembles your driver's license). Men: it will increase your responses 200%; women, by 100%.

One very clever man left me a personal ad voice mail message that he was sending me his photograph in the mail. The photo showed him sitting on a picnic table, and on the back he wrote the words, "I think you might be looking for me." His ingenuity was intriguing so his response got priority. (By the way, after three dates and many fun conversations we decided that we were too different and said good-bye.)

3. Never, ever, ever allow a man to pick you up at your home on the first date. Always meet in a mutually agreeable, neutral place, and drive yourself. One Midwest woman, who had had two 2-hour conversations with a man she thought fit her description of Mr. Right, invited a con-artist to her home and was subsequently date-raped. Fortunately, this man was apprehended. Men: Never suggest that you pick up a woman at her home nor push her to give you her home phone number or address until she feels totally comfortable. The same goes for you.

4. Best places to meet for the first time: car shows, flower shows, art shows, museums, etc. Try places where you can walk, talk, and get to know each other's tastes. Meeting for coffee is okay if it is a gourmet coffee spot, preferably in a bookstore.

5. Try to have at least three phone conversations before you meet. I have found that if people have undesirable qualities and behaviors you will get a good indication by the third call. Do not let the other party know that this is your requirement as they may interpret this as a challenge to make you give in.

6. Stay active with any socializing plan you have. Do something that you wanted to do anyway and you will not feel like you wasted your time by meeting someone who does not fit your realistic ideals.

7. Use careful wording on dating services' profiles or personal ads. However, the downside is that no matter what you ask for, some people will not pay attention. One of my research personal ads asked for a well-traveled successful entrepreneur, age 40-55, who preferred warmer climates. The ad netted many wonderful responses. I received one response from a 25-year-old aspiring

wrestler who had only been out of state once with his father. Though it was a sincere letter, it did not get a response due to age.

8. Do not expect a response from everyone. Remember that this is a numbers game where the odds are better than the lottery. If you "hit" on one out of 10-20 responses, that's great!

9. Leave a voice mail response *and* send a letter with your photo. This approach sets you above the rest, and gives you two opportunities to show how unique you are.

10. Give the personal ad holder plenty of time to respond. If s/he was swamped with responses, it will take time to call and meet everyone. Some people want to meet each person who responds before moving on to the next. I have heard of people taking up to 2-6 months to respond.

11. Letter responses: Men responding to women are braver in giving out their phone numbers and addresses. A post office box works fine.

12. Always send photos with personal ad responses. If you are concerned about how photogenic you are, go to a "glamour shot" photographer who will do your hair and makeup for you.

13. Save money on photographs: Go to a department store for photos or somewhere that will develop photos on the spot. Make color photocopies of the wallet size (copy the whole sheet) and use these to respond to personal ads. If you want your photo returned, include a self-addressed, stamped envelope.

14. Give as much information about yourself as possible. Tell the ad holder's voice mail key points about yourself and what you are looking for. Never answer an ad with, "Hi my name is Dave, please call me at --- ----." I never responded to such a generic, uncreative, message.

15. When responding to ads, use nice paper and try to personalize your response as much as possible.

16. Consider the quality of the publication in which you are placing your ad. Who is the target audience? Does the publication have a large circulation or readership? The Singles Press Association offers an ad for $175.00 that will be placed in approximately 16 papers nationwide including two specifically for Christians. Contact Ohio's Finest Singles at 216-521-1111 for more information.

17. The Internet and on-line computer services have personal ads and chat groups to meet people. Build up your relating skills on-line where you can flirt with little risk.

Personal Ads And Their Responses

> **Jan, petite 5'1", slim, likes plays, concerts.**
> **ISO (in search of) a tall, caring,**
> **financially secure man for dating.**

This is a fairly good ad. Almost anyone would qualify as "tall" since she is so short. But what age range is she looking for? She leaves us guessing. She wants him to be financially secure, so he'd better be able to take her to plays and concerts. Note: By "financially secure," most women mean a man who has a job and a decent car to drive, while most men interpret "financially secure" as being rich or extremely well off. I've known men who made $25,000 per year who were more generous and financially secure than men who made $40,000. Like age, salary is just a number. It's how you use it and how stable it is that women are concerned about.

> **Bob, 27, looking for SWF (single white female),**
> **18-35, under 150 lbs.**

Bob isn't interested in her finances, but weight is a concern (as it is for most men). However, most women would not answer this ad because he says nothing about himself.

> **Carol, 32, 5'6", brn hair, brn eyes, plus size,**
> **mother of 2 boys, ISO average M who enjoys**
> **camping, fishing trips, and is humorous,**
> **for lasting, loving relationship.**

Carol is definitely interested in a marriage partner and is open and honest about her size, children, and what she enjoys. By being truthful, she will get fewer replies, but they will be more genuine.

> **Ralph, likes going out and meeting people,**
> **line-dancing, and having fun.**

Ralph gives no age info, and he may be perfect for someone who wants a dancing partner. Based on this ad, you can assume he is playing the field and may not be interested in a committed relationship. What does he mean by "having fun"? Most women would be afraid this means sex right away.

> **SWF, 25, 5'11", brn hair, hzl eyes,**
> **ISO a fun guy to go out with.**

Dear SWF: Your ad may draw a lot of responses but beware: "fun" may be interpreted as "easy." This ad is too generic; fun is different for everyone, from bowling and chess tournaments to bungee jumping. It would be better to ask for someone with a fun attitude and tell more about yourself.

> **Mark, 5'6", 130 lbs, blonde/blue,**
> **very physically fit, good family values,**
> **hopeless romantic, down to earth,**
> **likes travel, dining out, dancing, comedy clubs.**

Hey Mark: You seem like a catch, but how old are you? At 5'6"/130 lbs., he's a lightweight and definitely wants someone else who's fit. He has a sense of humor and won't expect you to cook all the time. "Family values" might mean he's ready to settle down. He likes to dance so he must be somewhat confident and definitely not a couch potato. Who could resist this ad? I hope he really is romantic. My only other question would be whether he's been married before. This ad will generate many more responses than the previous ads listed.

> **Miss Excitement, Where are you?**
> **Nice-looking male 63, 5'10",**
> **enjoys dancing, having fun and enjoying life.**

Normally I would not recommend asking for "Miss Excitement," but in this case, since he's 63, it's great! He's obviously active and will get many responses. Catchy ad.

> **Ladies: Tired of being hit on by lounge lizards?**
> **Non-reptilian SBM, 40's, 5'6", no dependents.**
> **Prof. educator, master's degree plus.**
> **Enjoys most indoor activities.**
> **Seeking compatible, slender to med. build**
> **woman in 30's with no dependents or**
> **1 small child for relationship,**
> **possible marriage & family.**
> **Prefer woman who is easy to get along with,**
> **who takes pride in her femininity,**
> **and who doesn't use the word "like"**
> **in every sentence. Will travel.**

Very thorough ad, open minded, really interested in settling down, never married, flexible re: slender to med. build. You'd better have an education (I'd say at least a college degree) or I wouldn't recommend answering. "Will travel" may mean he's willing to drive to cities close by or fly to your state.

DWF, 40, 5'3", 120#, average attractive, brn hair/eyes NS/ND (non-smoker/non-drinker) quiet, artistic, outdoor lover. Likes movies, sunsets, picnics, quiet evenings, day trips, dining, compassion and more.
I have herpes (regrettably). I'd like to find a caring gentleman with the above qualities for friendship and possible lasting relationship.

This is an honest ad and a great way to find someone else who has had herpes. Imagine having a sexually transmitted disease that shows up several times a year and having to break the news to someone you've met any other way. 5'3" and 120 lbs. means she's an average size. She must have an auditory life strategy. . . she mentioned "quiet" twice (see "Mating" section for more on life strategies). She sounds laid-back yet active.

Note: What hasn't been mentioned in these ads are photo requirements. If you are going to play the personal AD-venture game, photos are a must. Many shopping malls have reasonable photo studios where you can get wallet size photos in an hour. No excuses.

> **ME: 33, brn/hazel, physically active, 6'+, slim,**
> **intense, goal oriented, passionate and kinesthetic.**
> **I like participating in sports, self-improvement, laughing,**
> **animals, long walks, sunsets, the outdoors.**
> **I don't live life looking in the rear view mirror.**
> **YOU: attractive, brunette, not overweight, physically active okay**
> **but not necessary. You must like yourself,**
> **be secure within yourself and not tied to the past;**
> **open, caring, kinesthetic a talkative free spirit who**
> **likes animals. GOAL: friendship leading to marriage.**

This ad should get plenty of qualified responses. He probably takes a lot of seminars, reads self-help books, and has a lot of pets (animals are mentioned twice). He's eliminated some emotional baggage in life and will be a partner you can grow with. He's obviously into Neuro-Linguistic Programming as he talks about being kinesthetic (twice), probably referring to his love strategy. Most people with kinesthetic life strategies aren't into sports and being very physically active. My guess is that he has a visual life strategy and a kinesthetic love strategy (see "Mating" section for more on love strategies).

> **Frank, 32, 6'3", 195 lbs., brn/hazel good-looking**
> **ISO honest F, 18-25, to go out and have fun with.**
> **No head games.**

Unlike the previous ad, Frank's shows some previous wounds. Don't we all want honest people? "No head games" means he's been hurt. Third clue: he wants a "fun," non-committed relationship. My guess is that he wants to take it really slow. Whoever ends up with Frank must deal with his last relationship, but at least you'll know what lies ahead.

Frank: spend more time telling us about you or we won't want to answer your ad. Who's he going to attract? Other women who've been burned.

Now, that you've checked out some do's and don'ts in personal ads, remember that how you describe yourself is no accident. You will also learn so much more from listening to the voice mail message and by reading any letters they send.

Tip: Buy some pre-stamped postcards to send to people who respond to your ad. Simply write, "Thanks for responding to ad # ___. I'll contact you later." Or, "Thanks for responding. Sorry, I'm already seeing someone." Or, "Thanks for responding. Sorry, you're not my type." If you're answering an ad yourself, expect that some people will never get in touch with you. It's easier for some people than rejecting you in any other way. P.S. Do not include your return address on the postcard. If they did not leave you an address in their initial response, then call their phone number and leave a message when you think they might not be home.

**Feisty, independent red head, attractive, age 33
DWF seeks financially secure entrepreneur,
age 38-55 who's health and personal-growth
oriented who'd be interested in relocating to Hawaii.**

This ad generated many quality responses, including people who were only thinking about being an entrepreneur.

Voice Mail Responses

Don't forget to record a warm voice mail box greeting. Write the script out beforehand and practice to make it seem spontaneous. When you leave a message for someone else, give plenty of reasons for them to contact you.

Below are examples of two wonderful responses:

Hi Sandra, this is Steve. You have a great voice. I'm 41, 6 feet tall, 180 pounds, and attractive. I have brown hair and blue eyes and really appreciate articulate women. I own my own business and am somewhat of a dilettante. Life is an adventure to share with someone special. I enjoy life. Call me at --- ---- so we can see if there's any chemistry between us.

Hi George, this is Sylvia. I just listened to your ad and couldn't help replying. I'm 5'5", average weight, blond with brown eyes. I love sports like you do, and I have two small children. I'm a ticket taker on the turnpike and meet many people every day. I think it would be fun to meet you. You can leave me a message on my voice mail and I'll call you right back.

Hail to Dennis Thornton, who graciously provided his artistic talent with the illustrations found in this book. Once in a while one meets special angels in life, Dennis is one. He states "While reading and illustrating this book, I began to use the information and have now found my twin flame in life. We will be married in a place I call church, where five waterfalls converge in a bamboo forest. If it weren't for Susan's techniques, I would have put my heart in a little basket and not even bothered to love again. Susan is a faith healer for love."

Not only are they now married, but as of this printing, they have a beautiful baby girl!

Chapter Ten

High Maintenance Mates

Are You A "High-Maintenance Man or Woman"?

HE SAYS: "I'm leaving soon. I have a date with a bimbo."

SHE SAYS: "I don't know whether to hang up or throw up. Why are you going out with a bimbo when you could have asked *me* out?"

HE SAYS: "Because you're a high-maintenance woman."

SHE SAYS: "I maintain myself, thank you!" She hangs up.

She thinks: "High-maintenance? What does he mean by that? What about his $200-a-month helicopter lessons? And how much does it cost to maintain his three cars? I hope he enjoys being alone!"

He thinks: "If I see her for very long it might cost me a lot of money."

FICTION: All women look for a man with lots of money.
FACT: *Women look for security, not lots of money. Men look for sex appeal and comfort.*

FICTION: Women who wear lots of jewelry probably got it from a man and they will want me to buy them more.
FACT: *Most women pride themselves on being able to buy their own jewelry. However, a gift of jewelry from a man is a sign that he values this person in his life. (Wouldn't you rather she wore something you gave her?)*

FICTION: If a woman wears a ring on her left hand, she's probably married.

FACT: *Women like jewelry and wear it all over. If she is wearing the ring on her middle finger, it is more likely that she's not taken.*

TRUTH: **"High-maintenance" women come in five varieties:**
A. Emotionally Dependent
B. Financially Dependent
C. Semi High-Maintenance
D. High-Maintenance
E. Gold-Digger

Choose wisely. There is a cost and benefit to every type of relationship. Here's how to recognize the five types:

Type A: Emotionally Dependent

She is loving and kind, and she caters to you. But after the first date she needs and wants a lot of your time. She may call you three times or more in one day. She feels hurt if you don't spend more time with her and call often enough. She might frequently ask, "Do you really like me?" She finds it hard to make decisions and often asks for your advice. She may care more about what other people think about her than what she thinks of herself. True, she needs a lot of affection, but she will also lavish it on you.

Type B: Financially Dependent

She doesn't have a career, she's a perpetual student, or she never graduated from school. Perhaps she stayed home to care for children. She may never have balanced a checkbook. Still, many Type B's are frugal. Their contribution is in handling all of your needs and theirs, i.e. laundry, cooking, and cleaning. If you enjoy being the sole provider, and want a great home life, this is the gal for you.

Type C: Semi-High Maintenance

This type is a real gem. On the outside, she could appear to be high-maintenance. But when you look for other clues, you'll find a very special and unique person. She's attractive, takes care of herself physically, and wears moderate-to-expensive clothing and quality accessories. She prefers men who care enough about themselves to dress well, too, even on casual days (although a sweat suit is fine if it doesn't have holes and is *not* gray — unless you have gray hair). She wears jewelry she buys for herself, sometimes as souvenirs of the trips she's taken.

She doesn't expect a man to pay for everything all the time. On a trip she may pay at least the airfare, if not more. She appreciates even small gifts. She likes going to classy restaurants, but not every day of the week. Fun restaurants - like TGI Friday's, or Max's Deli, or that cute little diner down the street - are great. She works hard and likes to buy you gifts, too. (Type C's also come in a variety of attitudes, from conservative to bold and daring.)

Type D: High-Maintenance

This woman was either born with a silver spoon or worked for it herself. She wants you to live in the "best" neighborhood, drive a certain class of car, and attend the "right" events, so you will have something in common. If you already meet these requirements, then you don't need to classify this woman as "High-Maintenance."

These women have high standards. Like Type C's, they may prefer their salad dressing on the side and ask to have their meal prepared in a special way. However, they're appreciative. Both semi- and high-maintenance women are likely to combine beauty and brains. The result? Stimulating conversation, good business cohorts, savvy, and they are definitely aware of quality of living.

WARNING! Don't confuse Type D's with the "Gold-Digger." On the outside they may look alike, but there are differences in personality and background (values, environment, career path, and expectations).

Type E: Gold-Digger
This type will act condescendingly, but will usually be quite
attractive. She hangs out in bars with jewelry dripping from every
finger. When you take her out, she will insist on the finest restaurants
and order without regard for the cost, since, after all, you will be
paying for it. Gifts you give them must be just "right," or Type E's
will be put off (and they *will* expect gifts). You'll hear this type brag
loudly about what their boyfriends bought them or what trips he's
taken them on. (A Semi-High Maintenance type merely mentions
how much fun their trip was and how gorgeous the scenery was.)
Many Gold-Diggers act pretentiously and complain too much about
service, even if it was a minor *faux pas* by the waiter/waitress.

First impressions are lasting, so, a word to the wise: All first dates
should be a little extra-special — a nice restaurant or event. Show her
a good time right away; later, you can do more relaxed things. Don't
offer to cook dinner for a first date unless you're a fabulous cook and
your home is clean and neat. (Most women would interpret a first date
at your place as a sign that you just want to show them your
"etchings" — if you know what I mean! Save this for later, or she'll
turn you down for fear of being in a compromising situation.) P.S.
Thoughtful women will cook dinner for you in return (unless they
don't know how to cook and order Chinese take out instead).

**A palace without affection is a poor hovel,
and the meanest hut with love in it
is a palace for the soul.**

-- Ingersoll

The Truth About Men, $, And Gold Diggers

There are a lot of lonely men out there. No matter how much, or how little, money they control, they share one fear: that women only want them for their financial assets. Some men are so afraid that they become tightwads and make it a point to avoid spending a dime on the opposite sex.

Men should know that *it's not, and I repeat NOT, how much you have that turns a woman on — it's how you use it* (which is also true for certain anatomical parts!). A woman would rarely love you *just* for your money.

Women are usually the partner who chooses whom they will end up with. Therefore, it's important to know that women qualify men in various ways. Check out these tips on how most women choose with whom they will spend their time.

- Most women would like to find someone who is at least as well off as they are, and not a deadbeat.

- Seeing men flash the cash strikes women as arrogant. This is important because women, even if they aren't aware of it, base desirability on "mate-ability." They look for qualities that will be desirable in the long-term and which will endure the test of time, either in marital or non-marital bliss.

- Women desire men who are confident and who understand the world of finance. This gives them a sense of security. Most prefer someone with a proven track record, as opposed to the "big gambler" type.

- You can be as poor as a church mouse, having "lost it all" in a recession, divorce, or some other situation, and it's possible to find a woman who will stand by you and support you in the rebuilding process.

Sad-But-True Story: One man I interviewed, told me about an acquaintance who had spent most of his years worrying that the women he met were after his money. Now, he says, his friend is "all alone and too old even to make love if he found the right woman."

What are the morals of this story?

1. Accept that women look for security. A good friend once said, "Never try to argue with or change a woman; it'd be easier to bail out the ocean!"

2. Women should likewise accept that, as a man is more desirable when his personal qualities are coupled with financial stability, women are indeed more desirable to men if they take care of themselves physically, paying attention to their shape, form, and overall attractiveness.

3. Practice simple prosperity consciousness. Act consistently with abundance, not scarcity. Leave decent tips. Send cards and flowers; create special times — life is too short not to! Consider the woman or man in your life as a partner for creating more wealth and enjoyment.

4. Men: The next time you hear yourself worrying about women and money, STOP. . . and do the opposite. Buy her a token of your appreciation (a book she wants, a gift certificate for a facial, etc.). **The reward will be worth the investment!**

5. It's the sum total of all of your qualities that makes you desirable to the opposite sex.

6. Generosity will make you feel better about yourself. Those who worry about people using them for their money undermine their own ability to judge character. In other words, they are saying to themselves and others that they can be duped. Time is a good test of any friendship.

One man told his date, "I have a car that gets me around. I hope it lasts until next year!" Yet he owns several successful businesses and drives a new Porsche! His remark seems like an insecure response as well as purposeful deception. Men: remember that most women ask about your car because they know how important it is to you. They often regard choice of car and how well it is maintained as a sign of stability and how much a man values himself.

7. Although women make more money now than in the past, men are still the major bread-winners. Single mothers may not always be able to return the favor of dinner, but there are other ways that considerate women will use to reciprocate or show they care. Look for them.

You may find these quotes from women interesting.

An experienced business woman stated: "Since I am successful, it's very important to me that a man be just as successful and powerful. I want these qualities in a man to balance and bring out my femininity. Men who haven't reached my financial level don't seem to understand me. They make me out to be a sergeant in the army rather than the *woman* that I really am. I'd like my financial success to be considered as a man is, just part of the package."
— *Carolyn, NY*

"A man who earns the same amount of money or more than I do will also have compatible interests in how we spend it. He'll understand why I insist on a weekly treat for both of us."
— *CPA, Cleveland*

"My marriage only lasted six months. We began to fight about money and it became very clear that neither of us was wrong; we just didn't have the same money values. I would rather spend a certain percentage of our income on vacations and investments. He insisted

on eliminating vacations. Life is too short! Find someone with similar beliefs, or one who is willing to compromise."
— *Attorney,* Dallas

"I am a secretary and will probably never make the kind of money a man does. It's very important to me that the man I marry have a good potential for taking care of a family."
— *Diane, Erie, PA*

To quote super-model, Cindy Crawford: "Passion is the sexiest thing you can see in someone. He can be this nerdy real estate guy, but when he starts talking passionately about deal-making, he becomes very sexy."

Top Six High Maintenance Men

Yes, Men can be High Maintenance too!

1. Men with expensive tastes who can't seem to hold down a job.

2. Men who want to be waited on hand and foot and demand your attention all the time.

3. Men who want a woman as an ornament to show off, and expect her to keep a perfect figure and look good all the time.

4. Jealous, possessive men.

5. Men who use the excuse "I forgot or I didn't hear you, too much.

6. Men who believe sex is the woman's job and want it all the time.
(**More details on High Maintenance Men can be found in the Companion Guide.)**

How to Be Irresistible - ♥ ~~~~~~~~~~~~~~> *103*

Chapter Eleven
Playing Cat and Mouse-The "REAL" Rules:

Relationships are much like playing tag, hide-and-seek, or cat-and-mouse. For a while you're "it". . . and then you're not. Sometimes the more disinterested you act, the more the opposite sex wants, and the harder they try. But as soon as you become interested, they seem to run in the opposite direction. This can be frustrating! As someone once said **"No one understands the boy/girl stuff, not even God!"** But there are two roles to play in this game: pursued and pursuer.

Act I: Being Pursued

1. Be willing to play.

2. Be willing to be "it."

3. Have fun being interested one moment, the next moment, not (it creates the chemistry of mystery).

4. Wait two days to see who calls first.

5. Just when things get "comfortable," act indifferent.

6. Just when the other person is about to give up trying, let him/her know just how crazy you are about him/her. (Enjoy this for a while.)
    Wake up guys! Sometimes women try everything to please you, and show you how much they care, until they are so discouraged that they quit trying. The instant she quits, the man decides she's like oxygen to him, and he can't live without her. But by then, it's too late.

7. Notice when it's your turn to be the pursuer.

Caution: Be subtle. Don't let this get to the point of no return, or you could lose this person!

Act II: The Pursuer

1. Now the shoe is on the other foot. Call frequently.

2. Send cards, flowers, or small surprises.

3. Spend extra time thinking just how special this person is and how much fun you will have together.

4. Notice that special feeling you have as you fantasize about how wonderful it would be if it were only you two together doing fun things forever! Do this often.

5. If you feel a little nervous that the other person might not reciprocate, don't deny this feeling. It will drive you to do more and to justify that your date is worth it.

6. Notice that your date is becoming more responsive, romantic, and interested. (Enjoy this for a little while.)

7. When you find yourself bored, ask yourself if this relationship is really what you want.

8. Repeat Act I.

Note: Remember to flirt with your potential relationship, even after it becomes long-term. Use these "rules" the rest of your life, even if you are married.

A good friend once said, "A relationship is like oxygen. We use it and breathe it every day and take it for granted until it's gone or threatens to go away and then we realize we can't live without it."
This "cat-and-mouse" game is the see-saw or ebb and flow of life. Trust it. It will balance out in the end if you're willing to accept it the way it is. As crazy as these "rules" seem, don't let them drive you crazy! It's like playing baseball. You'd get bored, too, if you always played the batter, or always played outfield.

Like any game, it's not whether you win or lose, but how you play the
_ _ _ _. One second you're in love. . . and the next, you're not. That's
just the way love is. Relax and enjoy these cycles of love, while
learning and growing together.

FACT: We do more for our careers than our relationships. We go
to school, take classes, work hard, work late, put up with a
lot, and butter up the boss and her husband.

FACT: Even a great career can't make up for a miserable
relationship.

FACT: A great relationship makes a boring or intolerable job less
painful.

EYE CONTACT
Obviously, A Flirting Technique That Works.

Mating

Rituals of Courtship: Chemistry,
Compatibility, Romance, and
Irresistible Mate Selection

ᗰop ᗰen ℛules of Irresistibility

1. Be, think, act and dress irresistibly.

2. Treat everyone around you as if they, too, are irresistible.

3. Smile a lot. A smile is the best thing you can wear. Show teeth.

4. Imagine sending people you are interested in a mental hug. Do it with a twinkle in your eye.

5. Make people feel comfortable around you.

6. Take action. Introduce yourself. "Hi, I noticed you. (Don't wait for a verbal response — keep going.) I couldn't pass up the opportunity to introduce myself. Since there is no one here to properly introduce us, I'll do the honors."

7. Get beyond the 5-10 second silence that usually occurs right after meeting or speaking for the first time. Ask questions to find things that you have in common.

8. Do not stay and talk all night to the same person. Act like a dragonfly and visit for a while, leave and come back for more.

9. Discover what you would spend your life doing if you didn't have to work, cook, clean, if you already had a dream house, and you could travel anywhere you wanted to go. What would you do?

10. Remember that you will not be "Irresistible" to everyone, all the time. Maintain a basic level of "Irresistibility", and learn how to pour it on whenever you want. (An expanded and more detailed version of this list is found in the Companion Guide.)

Chapter Twelve

Love and Attraction Strategies

Read at your own risk!

When we feel loved, our brain releases certain chemicals into our body. One of these chemicals is oxytocin. Women can produce oxytocin simply from being cuddled, which may explain why many women prefer cuddling and hugging to sex. Oxytocin is released when people around us accidentally hit upon our love strategy. They may unknowingly **say** the right words in just the right way, or **touch** us gently in the right place, or **show** us something that unleashes those powerful feelings of *amour*. The love strategy is usually a combination and certain order of all three. Each of us have our own personal combination and order which causes us to feel loved.

The combination consists of three simple secrets: seeing, hearing, and feeling clues, also known as visual, auditory, and kinesthetic clues. Of course, we all need to see, hear, and feel that we are loved. But the order of importance differs from person to person. The key to the combination is in knowing which order is the right one for you and anyone special in your life. (Unlocking the order is easy. Simply listen to yourself and others as they describe the times that they felt really loved, touched, or moved.)

The above applies to non-romantic relationships, too. Discover your mother's or father's love strategy and your relationship will see a decrease in conflicts and an increase in communication. Suddenly, they may feel as if you "really understand." Uncover your boss' or co-worker's love/appreciation strategy and they will feel appreciated and be more cooperative. You'll be able to speak their "language." P.S. Your romantic interests will soar!

Now that you know some of the benefits, let's get down to the how-to's.

What is Your Love ♥ Strategy?
(Note: Use this same process to discover
Attraction Strategies too!)

1. Begin by remembering a time when you felt that special feeling of being "loved" or when you had special feelings for another person. (Choose a strong memory.)

2. What was happening at that moment? Did you see or hear something special, or was it the touch of someone or something you remember most?

3. As you remember what made you feel loved, ask yourself these questions: Was it the sound of the voice, the words of a letter, a mental picture of the event, or a special gift someone gave you? Was it an embrace or gentle touch that made you feel special?

4. To see, hear, and feel love are needs we all have, but one of these needs will be *most* important to you. When that need is met, you will feel especially loved. Which one is key for you? Another way to determine your most important need is to think about what was missing the most in your last relationship? Was there not enough conversation, touching, attention, or gifts/flowers?

5. For now, just find the need that is most important to you. You'll figure out the exact percentage of visual, auditory, kinesthetic needs and the order of importance later on. You may already know that you would prefer to have someone **tell** you rather than **show** you how much they love you; or, you may need their **touch** to feel loved.
   For example, one of my clients had a Love ♥ Strategy combination in this order: first, "feeling"; second, "hearing"; and third, "seeing." This meant his girlfriend would (if she really

wanted to make him feel special): **first**, hug him for more than five seconds when he came home from work; **second**, tell him how much she missed him; and **third** (the most minor part of the combination), show him by doing something (for example, polishing his shoes). In return, assuming he knew her combination and really cared about her, he would fulfill her Love ♥ Strategy.

Love ♥ Strategy Clues

Clue: If someone you care about spends a lot of time sending letters and notes to you, or they call you often, you can almost bet that they need to "hear" they are loved through your tone of voice, how often you call, how long you talk and notes you send, etc. This is an example of a strong Auditory Love ♥ Strategy.

Clue: When someone complains that you "never" tell them how much you care, or that you "never" call them — or don't really listen — they have an Auditory Love ♥ Strategy, meaning the first key to their combination is hearing.

Clue: If you enjoy receiving flowers and little gifts, and like it when someone does things for you, or if you notice that this is how your significant other shows love to you and others, then this is a good indication of a love strategy that is primarily "visual" or "seeing."

Clue: If the first thing you or your loved one wants when you come home is that long hug or kiss (not a peck but a 4-5 second kiss), this points to a "kinesthetic" or "feeling" Love ♥ Strategy.

Clue: Often people ask me how a card or note can be considered *both visual and auditory*. If a card's emphasis is on the picture rather than the words, or if the words used draw a picture, it is a visual card. A card with more writing than graphics is auditory. If the card's paper is very textured, and the words are feeling-oriented, it will appeal to someone more kinesthetic. Like cards, flowers are a pretty universal way of showing you care. Always remember to include a special note when giving them to someone with an auditory love strategy or they won't have as much impact.

Pinpoint Your Love ♥ Strategy.

Ask yourself the following questions. Devote plenty of time to the answers.

Remember your last or current relationship.
1. What makes/made it special for you?

2. What do you/did you enjoy and value the most?
    A. Was it what was said? How does/did that make you feel?
    B. Was it how you were touched? How does/did that make you feel?
    C. Was it something you saw him/her doing for you or some other visible way to "see" love?

3. What was or is missing in the relationship for you? What did you want or need more of?

Next, ask yourself these questions:
1. If my partner were not able to communicate with me (i.e. talk, have long conversations, use sign language, or write letters), would I be able to really feel loved?
    If you answered no, then you have an auditory need to be loved.

2. If s/he neglected to bring me any tokens or gifts of love, never took me out, or forgot to notice how I look, would I take that as a big sign that they didn't love me?

    If you answered yes, then you have a visual love strategy. If you are the kind of person that eagerly awaits visible signs of loving (blowing a kiss, gifts, etc.) and are disappointed to the point of feeling unloved when you don't receive them, consider your major Love ♥ Strategy to be visual.

3. If s/he could never touch me again, (i.e., had to live in another country without visitation rights), would I know I was loved even if s/he wrote and called frequently?

   If you answered "no" to this question you have a feeling Love ♥ Strategy. Someone with a feeling or kinesthetic Love ♥ Strategy might know in theory that they are loved, but would not feel it. Without their "feeling need" being met, this relationship would not succeed for very long.

Repeat the questions if necessary until you narrow down your answers into the three categories in order of importance: feeling/kinesthetic, hearing/auditory, or seeing/visual. Have fun with this! In the next section you'll learn how to discover others' strategies so you can give them the hugs, verbal assurance or visible loving that they need. Watch your partners respond and relationships grow. Don't forget to ask for what *you* need, too.

More on Love ♥ Strategies

Now that you have figured out your own Love ♥ Strategy, it's time to discover someone else's. How does your potential significant other know when someone loves them? How does s/he show love to others? Begin by looking for evidence of the three different strategies and find out how your partner knows that they are totally loved. Most people think of a strategy as a plan to get something or somewhere. Using a Love ♥ Strategy will not get you anything, but it will make the people around you feel more loved and loving.

Your love strategy needs will be one of the following :

Telling (via long conversations, tone of voice, frequent phone calls, verbal assurance) = AUDITORY

Showing (with flowers, going out a lot, cards with pictures rather than words, gifts). = VISUAL

Feeling (through touch, hugs, spending "enough" time with each other)= KINESTHETIC

Though each of us needs all three forms of assurance that we are loved, one matters most; when it is missing, the relationship becomes precarious. When we first start seeing someone new, all three needs are usually met. Think about it: in the beginning of any relationship, you go through a mutual discovery process. You may find yourselves talking a lot more than usual, sometimes having long conversations into the night (AUDITORY). You'll probably go out to many different places — shows, parties, restaurants, etc. (VISUAL). There is also a lot of touching — holding hands, hugs, kisses (KINESTHETIC). Intimate relations are always more frequent in the first few years of a relationship.

Because all three needs are being met in the initial stages of the dating and mate selection process, our Love ♥ Strategy gets triggered constantly. As time goes on, the relationship settles down and *we tend to love our special someone in the way that we need to be loved.* For example: If we love books, we give books as presents to show our affection. If we love back rubs, we give back rubs. If we love music, we give gifts of music or want to spend a significant amount of time enjoying music with our partner.

CONFLICT will occur when couples have different love strategies and do not know how to fulfill them.

She: You just don't love me like you used to.

He: What do you mean? I haven't changed. I **tell** you all the time how much I love you.

She: Yes, but you never **take** me anywhere, and you used to **send** me cards and flowers. What happened to that?

He: Nothing has changed. I **call** to tell you how much I care every night. I **say** I love you, but I never **hear** you say it to me.

She: I **show** you all the time.

The above conversation would happen between a woman with a visual love strategy and a man with an auditory love strategy. She obviously needs to be *shown* love, while he needs *verbal assurance*. Until each of them realizes what the other needs, neither of them will be happy or satisfied. The most compatible strategies are matched, e.g. visual-visual, auditory-auditory, and kinesthetic-kinesthetic (feeling). However, you can make almost any combination work harmoniously once you become aware of your needs and your partner's. P.S. These principles work well in non-romantic, family, and friendship relations, too!

Life Strategies™ vs. Love ♥ Strategies

Just because someone acts primarily visual in everyday life does not mean that they have a Visual Love ♥ Strategy. If you are familiar with Neuro-Linguistics or if you have read any of Tracy Cabot's books on relationships, take note: Those books lead the reader to believe that if someone is visual, they have a visual love strategy. The mode (visual, auditory or kinesthetic) in which s/he operates in life may not be the same mode as their love strategy. I have coined the phrase "Life Strategy™" to distinguish between the two.
Life is all that happens to you. Your Life Strategy™ is how you interpret all that happens to you, the color of the lenses through which

you view life. For some, it is a conglomeration of pictures; for others sounds, and for the rest; it is feelings and emotions. While all three modes (visual, auditory, and kinesthetic) are valuable, human beings tend to pay attention to and use one mode more than another.

A Life Strategy™ greatly differs from a Love ♥ Strategy. A Life Strategy™ is the combination of a visual, auditory and kinesthetic orientations that we use to survive in our daily lives. It is our own winning formula, a way we are thrown toward behaving and reacting. Your Life Strategy™ will be more apparent when you are under stress. When I'm under stress, I use my visual sense first to solve problems. I want things to look a certain way in order for them to feel right. My life partner's Life Strategy™ is Auditory — he talks to himself and must have control over his "hearing" environment. Things need to sound right for him to feel in control.

Ask These Questions to Figure Out A Life Strategy™

To discover your own primary life strategy ask yourself the following questions and pay close attention to the type of words you use in forming your answers.

1. Describe your favorite forest. If your forest could be anyway you wanted, what would it be like?
   Notice your response. Did you describe colors and what the forest looks like? For example: light is beaming between the trees, there are flowers everywhere. (VISUAL).
   Did you describe how you would feel in your fantasy forest? For example: the forest is peaceful, warm, spacious. (FEELING/KINESTHETIC).
   Did sounds predominate the description? For example: there are rustling leaves and a babbling brook. (AUDITORY).

2. Describe your dream car (a great exercise for men).
   If you love the sound of the engine, think AUDITORY.
   If the color and shape are more important, think VISUAL.
   If you are drawn to the comfort and smooth ride, think KINESTHETIC.

3. Describe your dream house (a great exercise for women).
Did you think of the color of the house and describe in detail how
the furniture is arranged? Think VISUAL.

Did you emphasize the size and coziness? Think KINESTHETIC.

Did you describe the quiet cul-de-sac where you live, the sounds
of the nearby ocean, or the great stereo system, think
AUDITORY.

Effects of Life and Love ♥ Strategies
On Compatibility

*Use this section to determine your life and love strategies and to
learn more about which type of person you would be most compatible
with.*

Life Strategy™   Love ♥ Strategy

Type 1: Life-Visual (LV)   **Love-Visual (♥V)= LV-♥V**
This person needs to live in a beautiful environment, likes things to
look a certain way, really cares about clothes, and will be able to
determine how much you care if you appreciate these things, too, and
give visual gifts. They need to spend time with you doing visual
activities like going to "see" things (movies, sightseeing, window-
shopping, views, places with a lot of people). Make sure they get the
chair with the most scenic view. This person needs the least amount
of touching and alone time with their significant other.
*Most compatible with Types 2, 4, and then 3 in that order. Note:
those who share the same strategy (LV - ♥V) may have conflict unless
they agree on how things should look.*

Type 2: Life-Visual (LV)   Love-Auditory (♥A)= LV-♥A

This person is similar to the above with these exceptions: S/he needs more conversations and knows they are loved by what you say and how often you say "I love you," (or use other endearing terms).
Most compatible with own type, then with 4, 3, and 1.

Type 3: Life-Visual (LV)   Love-Kinesthetic (♥K)= LV-♥K

This person is similar to #1 except that the need to be touched is greater. Although a visual person is usually happy to "see" their partner from across the room, this type will need to occasionally touch and spend more time side by side with his/her partner.
Most compatible with own type, type 6, then types 7, 2 and 4.

Type 4: Life-Auditory (LA) Love-Visual (♥V)= LA-♥V

Those with this life strategy live in a world of sounds — those they like and those they don't like. It's easy to make this type squirm: tune the car radio so that the music has just a bit of static noise (one of their pet peeves). Auditory loved ones move at a slightly slower pace than Visuals and are more likely to have rhythmic movements. They tend to think a bit more than visuals before responding to questions and choose words carefully. If you are in love with this type, I hope you enjoy the same music! The ♥V (Love Visual) part is seen in giving gifts that can be seen and heard (CD's, tapes, tickets to concerts). Conversations with groups of people turn this type on.
Compatible with own type, then types 5, 2, and 6.

Type 5: Life-Auditory (LA) Love- Auditory (♥A)= LA-♥A

Double whammy here! Plan on spending a lot of time in one-to-one conversation without distractions. Call this person to say "I love you" and you'll be a hit. Communication is of the utmost importance. There can never be enough letters, or quick calls to check in. This type can sustain a long-distance relationship and still feel loved if there is enough telephone contact. Possible conflicts? The noises in your car that you don't even hear annoy this type; they will either love the sound of a passing train or hate it. If you go to visit this type of person and do not spend "enough" time actually talking to them they

will not feel loved. How much is "enough"? If they start to hint that they don't feel loved or want to talk more, you'll know they need more. Plan on sending plenty of cards to this type; a gift without a card is only one-half of a gift.
Compatible with own type, then types 6, 8 and 2

Type 6: Life-Auditory (LA) Love-Kinesthetic (♥K)= LA-♥K
This type (like most auditories) needs conversations as above but needs more time together with you and does not do as well in long-distance relationships or when you must travel for business. The ♥ Kinesthetic strategy demands time together, both with others and alone. Touch is very important.
Most compatible with own type then types 3, 8, 5, and 4.

Type 7: Life-Kinesthetic (LK) Love-Visual (♥V)= LK-♥V
(Very rare)
You'll recognize the "feeling" type because their clothes are designed for comfort, not looks. They'll choose the most comfortable cars, chairs, couches, and mattresses. This type moves much more slowly than the rest, and takes longer to respond to questions because they are checking out their feelings first. Life-Visuals get impatient with Life-Kinesthetics because they want them to be the same speed. LV's and LK's have more difficulty adjusting to their differences. The visual wants the couch to *look* a certain way (comfort is not very important), while the kinesthetic wants the couch to be *comfortable* at all costs. Feeling types love texture, things they can touch, textured wallpaper and stationery, etc. With a Visual ♥ Love Strategy they'll need touchable gifts more than types 8 and 9.
Compatible with own type and with types 8, 9, 4, and 6.

Change your thoughts and you will change your world.

Norman Vincent Peale

Type 8. Life-Kinesthetic (LK)   Love-Auditory (♥A)= LK-♥K

This person may be a touchy-feely type but demands time together talking. Words that express feelings give them warm fuzzies; e.g., "If I were there right now I would give you a warm, soft hug." This type does not want to spend much time away from you but gives great hugs and wants them back. These people tend to touch people often when talking.

Most compatible with own type, types 6, 9, 7, and occasionally type 3.

Type 9: Life-Kinesthetic (LK)   Love-Kines. (♥K)= LK-♥K

If you love closeness and lots of touching then this is the type for you. Type 9 prefers slow dancing to fast and lives to be with you, work with you, and do everything with you. Visuals feel smothered by this type. A visual prefers to spend a moderate amount of time with their partner at a party; but is happy as long as they can see their partner from across the room. Not so for the LK-♥K: To love this type is to spend time together with enough touching or they will experience what I call "skin hunger" and not feel loved.

Most compatible with its own type then types 8, 7, 6, and 5.

Compatibility Grid

Use this grid to determine whom you'd get along best with. Key:
1 = Most compatible
5 = Less compatible
No rating = not easily compatible
Find your type in the top row. Then look down the column vertically underneath your type to find your most compatible matches. For example, if you are type 3 — LV ♥K (Life Strategy™ Visual and Love ♥ Strategy Kinesthetic), you will be most compatible with someone who is LV♥K (noted by the number 1), the second most compatible with LA♥K (noted by the number 2), and so on. If there is no rating, assume that compatibility is poor to none.

Remember that the L denotes Life Strategy™ and the ♥ denotes Love Strategy. Either strategy can be primarily V for Visual, A for Auditory or K for Kinesthetic.

Type	1	2	3	4	5	6	7	8	9
Your Strategy	LV ♥V	LV ♥A	LV ♥K	LA ♥V	LA ♥A	LA ♥K	LK ♥V	LK ♥A	LK ♥K
LV ♥V	2	4							
LV ♥A	1	1	4	3	4				
LV ♥K	4	3	1			2		*5	
LA ♥V	3	2	5	1		5	4		
LA ♥A				2	1	4			5
LA ♥K			2	4	2	1	5	2	4
LK ♥V			3				1	4	3
LK ♥A					3	3	2	1	2
LK ♥K							3	3	1

* Only occasionally compatible.

Play with these concepts — you'll be surprised with the results. If you would like more assistance with these exercises, an 80 minute audio tape is available. Call 1-800 -Compatible (266-7284) or (216) 521-LOVE (5683).

Review the explanations of compatibility on the previous page. This is new information and will take a couple of tries to really "get it."

Fill in the following statements:

My Life Strategy is _____. My Love ♥ Strategy is _____.

I am most compatible with someone who has a
_____ Life Strategy™ and a _____ Love ♥ Strategy.

I am second most compatible with someone who has a:
_____ Life Strategy and a _____ Love ♥ Strategy.

My partner's primary Life Strategy is_____ and primary Love
Strategy is_____.

This means that I should _____
_____ to make him/her feel more loved.

**Try to get even with those
who've helped you the most.**

S.E.B.

Attraction ⇒ ⇐Strategies

It Takes Two to "Tangle"

Before figuring out attraction strategies, consider how we tangle. Take inventory of your past relationship skills. Have you ever thought that life might be easier without the opposite sex. . . and then realized how empty life is without someone to care about? Relationships can be a passionate nurturing force in our lives or a huge drain on our emotional reserves. Since it always takes more than one to participate, and attraction plays such a big part of it, look at your current or last romance.

If you are already in a relationship, does your "romance" feel more like a "ball and chain"? Have you both gotten into repeating patterns of communication, negative actions, upsets? Skip to paragraph 5 if this has never applied to you.

Are you hearing things like "You *always* this," and "You *never* that"? Maybe it's time to consider moving on to the next relationship or maybe you just need to learn more relationship skills. After all, none of us were born knowing how to have the perfect relationship. Ending an unhealthy relationship can be a painful prospect, but there are better alternatives. Most duos end in one giant blow-out. **People tend to think they need to *end* a relationship. A more healthy way, however, is to *complete* it.**

"Completing" a relationship means cleaning up loose ends, changing the status from intimate to less intimate, and usually includes spending less time with each other. Completion always means communicating and discussing past issues that are unresolved. Since the relationship is changing and you may be moving on, these discussions can be had without the emotional charge, without getting "plugged in" or having your buttons pushed.

Sometimes the relationship will renew itself during this process. This would indicate a need to "RESOURCE" the relationship. "Resourcing" means considering and remembering the beginning of the relationship. What made the two of you become an item? Do you remember when you noticed how attracted you were? Remembering your "Attraction Strategy" and learning how to spark the flames again, as well as discovering your partner's "Love Strategy," are new resources to redirect the quality and enjoyment in your current or future relationship to inspire it to a new, all-time high.

Attraction strategies consist of certain repeatable patterns which cause you to become attracted to someone.

For example: A person I interviewed was first visually attracted to the women he dated and later married. He was married twice, and though now divorced, he finds himself always behaving in the same ways: First he is attracted to what he sees; then he says something to himself like, "Hmmm, I like this one"; then his attraction grows only if he "hears" the woman talk in a certain feisty way towards him. Then he asks her out. In other words, first he is visual, then he says something to himself (auditory), then he hears something (auditory), which causes him to take action.

So, his strategy is V e - A i - A e which means: Visual (external) — what he saw; Auditory (internal) — what he said to himself ; then he heard something Auditory (external), which then triggered the "chemistry," or attraction strategy strongly enough for him to risk rejection enough to initiate meeting this person.

If you use the right strategy, it is even possible to tell a friend about someone you want them to meet that would make him/her impatiently await the introduction. However, the way someone describes the person s/he is interested in and what adjectives s/he might use — sweet, hot, debonair, etc. — are the other details of an Attraction Strategy. If your best friend's Attraction Strategy included finding someone with "kind eyes" and you described someone with "soulful eyes," your friend may not be interested.

The fun part about Attraction Strategies is that we can isolate the events and repeat them to keep our attraction alive and growing. The sad part is that some people end up in the wrong relationship just because someone accidentally triggered the attraction chemistry. These people thought the attraction had more meaning than it actually did. To learn more about these and other relationship skills, audio tapes and seminars are available.

Questions to Ask Your Partner to
Discover Their Attraction ⇒ ⇐ Strategy

1A. How did you meet your former spouse/girlfriend/boyfriend, etc.?(This one question will give you many clues.)

1B. What was the very first thing that you noticed about him/her?

2. What was the very first thing you noticed about me that made you want to get to know me?

3. What qualities did your former partner have that made you interested in him/her (e.g., sincerity, sense of fun, intelligence)?

4. What's your definition of the quality/ies mentioned in the previous question? For example, if you mentioned "sincere eyes," what's your definition of "sincere"? (This is important because everyone has different ways of assigning meaning.) Ask your partner how s/he would know when someone was being _____ (fill in the blank; e.g., "sincere" or had "sincere eyes."

Love is the only force capable of transforming an enemy into a friend.

-- Dr. Martin Luther King, Jr.

The supreme happiness of life is the conviction that we are loved.

-- Victor Hugo
Les Miserables (1862), Fantine, bk. V, ch. 4

ꝺop ꝺen Gift Giving ꝺips for ꝺWomen

10. **Jewelry, Jewelry, Jewelry!** If you are not in a committed relationship, give earrings or a necklace. Proceed with a ring only if this is someone whom you want to be with for a long while. (Exceptions: Give her a ring that is costume jewelry or that does not look like an engagement ring.)

9. **Clothing that fits!** Hint: Notice something she already wears, then look at the size on the tag when it's hanging in the closet or in the laundry basket. Ask one of her friends to find out what size she is. This will get you extra points because her friend will tell her you've been asking about sizes for gifts and she will get excited.

8. Gift certificates to her favorite stores — one size fits all.

7. A package for a day at a spa (usually includes pedicure, manicure, facial and/or massage, makeup application, and hair styling; half-day packages are also available).

6. Never give just lingerie. Although it is a romantic gift, she will want something to show you're interested in *her* and not just sex.

5. If she asks for a practical gift like a fax machine, always give her a little romantic gift, too. (This should be something personal — a pretty hair barrette, costume jewelry, perfume if it's her favorite type, a framed picture of yourself, a book she's been wanting.)

4. Never give her a toaster or a blender.

3. Never completely believe a woman when she says, "Please don't get me anything." She's still secretly hoping you will. It's an extra sign that you really care when you ignore that statement. **Tip:** Don't make it a large gift as this could upset her. Aim for a

medium-size gift that says, "I just couldn't resist getting the woman I adore something for (whatever occasion)." She'll forgive you.

2. Create mystery. Make a treasure hunt. Hide the gift and leave little notes or smaller gifts with notes attached that give clues for the best one.

1. Wrap it in a box that does not match the size of the gift. Or wrap it in multiple boxes each one wrapped beautifully.

If all else fails. . .hire a personal shopper.

**A lady's imagination is very rapid;
it jumps from admiration to love,
from love to matrimony in a moment.**

**-- *Jane Austen*
Pride and Prejudice (1813), ch. 6**

𝒯op 𝒯en Gift 𝒯ips 𝒻or 𝒨en

1. GADGETS, GADGETS, GADGETS!

2. Sports-related clothing and accessories.

3. Something he really wants (even if you think it's crazy).

4. Ask a buddy of his what he's been wanting.

5. Gift certificates handmade by you for back massages and other sensual surprises.

6. Flowers: send them to him work or at home. They send them to us, why shouldn't they know what it's like? Balloons work well, too.

7. Sports equipment.

8. Tickets to his favorite sporting event.

9. Something for his car.

10. Give him his own remote control with his initials on it.

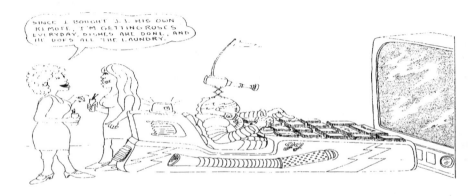

Chapter Thirteen

Getting Lucky: Romance 102

Romantic Ideas:
It's the Little Things That Count

Ever wanted more romance, or wanted to be romantic and didn't know how, didn't have enough time, money or energy? If you don't create some time for romance, you could end up very lonely and unhappy. Please note the following time-saving ideas.

Emergency Phone #'s for the Romantically Impaired
Order from catalogs and 800 numbers.
Most keep later hours and will even deliver overnight!

1-800-374-5505: The Red Rose Collection — the most irresistible catalog of them all — has tons of amazing gift ideas. This catalog is so beautiful, you'll want to have it just to look at!

1-800-LDROSES (1-800-537-0737): One of my personal favorites! $49.99 sends a dozen roses overnight. Call 9 a.m. - 7 p.m. EST Monday - Friday, 10 a.m. -2 p.m. Saturday, or fax your order (1-800-FAX-LOVE [1-800-329-5683]). **Tip:** Try their special fire-n-ice roses or designer mauve!

1-800-COMPATIBLE (1-800-266-7284): Increase your intimacy. Buy the video "Sacred Sex"($30 + S/H) and you'll both benefit. Set the scene with candles and flowers, and plan to spend plenty of time together enhancing your love life.

1-800-ASK-MALLEYS (1-800-275-6255) Truffles. Kisses. The Word LOVE. Chocolate Covered Pretzels. Chocolate Tool Kit. Golf Balls. Corvette. Antique Car or Cellular Phone. Spend $200 min. for your own design mold. 8:30am - 11:00pm EST.

1-800-FLOWERS (1-800-356-9377): No more excuses! Order 24 hours a day, seven days a week.

1-800-325-6000: For a special occasion or an "I love you" message, send a Western Union Telegram (by messenger, phonogram, or overnight mail).

1-800-527-6566: Celebration Fantastic — another beautiful catalog with romantic gifts. Call 8 a.m. - 5 p.m. PST. If you have their catalog you can order 24 hours a day.

She says: "My husband travels a lot on business. Why does he always find time for sex, but no time for romance? The way I see it, no romance = no sex!"

He says: "Why would my wife think I cheat on her when I'm on my trips? I love her so I wouldn't want to, and I do not have time to cheat."

The answer: You are not meeting her Love and Attraction Strategies. Give these Romance Tips a try.

No Cost - Low Effort Romance Ideas

1. Write little messages and freeze inside ice cubes or stuff inside a clear balloon with a colorful ribbon.

2. Compliment him/her every three hours.

3. Leave a coupon good for a free back or foot massage (30-min.)

4. Mail a coupon inside a beautiful/funny homemade card good for one distasteful chore (car wash, clean bathroom, run errands).

5. Leave ten little notes all over the house, in the car, underwear drawer, refrigerator, etc.

6. Light a candle in the living room. Take him/her by the hand and say, "This time is just for us." You figure out the rest.

7. After spreading low-fat butter or jam (or Nutella — yum!) on a piece of toast, use the end of a knife to draw a heart or write "I

love you" and hand it to your loved one. Or, tear/cut the toast into the shape of a heart.

Gift Giving Tips
1. Make a list of ten things you know s/he would love.

2. Prepare for shopping. Do you know his/her sizes? Find out *and write them down. Use the handy form in the Companion Guide.*

3. Mark all significant dates on your appointment calendar with a one-week advance notice reminder.

4. Buy gifts at least one week in advance.

5. Shop from catalogs!

Catalog Ideas
1. Have your partner start a Dream Book notebook with pictures of things s/he wants someday but wouldn't spend the money on right now. Make sure the phone number from the catalog is marked next to the picture so you or your partner can order easily. Include everything from jewelry to kitchen gadgets to books to crystals (in all price ranges in your book.) Whenever you or your loved one needs gift ideas, look in the Dream Book and order away.

2. Call **1-800-315-1995** to order the Shop At Home Catalog Directory. You'll find catalogs for everything!

3. Lillian Vernon Catalogs —**1-800-285-5555**. I find at least 5-10 things I want in every catalog they send me.

4. Playboy Gifts Catalog — **1-800-423-9494**: classy & innovative gifts for both sexes.

5. Victoria's Secret - **1-800-888-8200**: Choose from their array of lingerie or send a gift certificate. Women love their lotions and cologne.

Just for Men

1. If you really want to knock her off her feet , **wear a tux home from work...** and watch her face light up with surprise. Or go shopping with her and when she sees an outfit she'd really love, wait until she returns to the dressing room, pay for the outfit, walk back to the dressing room with scissors, cut off the tags and whisper in her ear that she can wear the outfit home! Prepare for wide eyes and jaw dropping. She'll be talking about this one forever.

2. Buy loose rose petals from a florist and spread them all over the breakfast table or at any restaurant (or on bed sheets). They're satiny and look so special.

3. Did you know that you can rent a few minutes on the giant electronic sign on Times Square in New York City for approximately $195.00? You just have to make sure your loved one is on the right corner at that time. I've heard it's been used for marriage proposals and birthday greetings.

For Women Only

1. Men love gadgets, electronic gifts, and practical gifts. Don't just buy them the things you want them to have, buy them the things *they want*, no matter how boring or unromantic it seems to you.

2. Give a gift certificate for a professional massage.

3. Give a fantasy boudoir photo of yourself.

4. Wear lingerie when he comes to pick you up on a date you've arranged. (I hope you know him that well.)

5. Do something with him you hate to do, i.e. watch the game, go bowling, fishing, etc., but remember to do it with a smile and without grumbling even once. Who knows — you might learn something new or even find you like it!

Romance Tips, Tips, Tips!

- Observe all mandatory holidays for gift giving, i.e. Sweetest Day, Valentine's Day, birthdays, anniversaries, Christmas, Hanukkah, etc. Get with the program — the misery of forgetfulness is not worth it. Romance is more appreciated when you give gifts, surprises, and do special things in everyday life, too!

- *Don't wait for a special occasion, make it a special occasion! The rewards are worth it.*

- P.S. For more romance ideas than I can give you here, purchase Greg Godek's books: *1001 Ways to Be Romantic* or *1001 More Ways to be Romantic.*

- Send her/him a handwritten note with some poetry, an expression, or a quotation that tells how you feel. Here's one of my favorites:

**She walks in beauty, like the night
Of cloudless climes and starry skies;
And all that's best of dark and bright
Meet in her aspect and her eyes:
Thus mellow'd to that tender light
Which heaven to gaudy day denies.**

**-- Lord Byron
Hebrew Melodies (1815). She Walks in Beauty, st. 1**

**We attract hearts by the qualities we display;
we retain them by the qualities we possess.**

-- Jean Baptiste Antoine Suard

ᴼᴼᴼop ᴼᴼᴼen ᴿomantic ᴼᴼideos

1. "Pretty Woman"

2. "Casablanca"

3. "An Affair to Remember"

4. "Ghost"

5. "Romancing the Stone"

6. "Always"

7. "Dr. Zhivago"

8. "Sleepless in Seattle"

9. "Gone With the Wind"

10. "Don Juan DeMarco"

Alternates:

"Barefoot in the Park"

"Charade"

"Notorious"

"The Ghost and Mrs. Muir"

"The Bridges of Madison County"

"French Kiss"

Chapter Fourteen

Intimacy is Closer than Sex!

Intimacy. . . sex. . . two words that are often confused with each other. We all know what sex is, but let me remind you of the definition of intimacy. *Webster's Dictionary* defines intimacy as "a close or familiar association, usually an affectionate or loving, personal relationship. . . a private, closely personal, detailed, or deep relation-ship; showing a close union, an innermost and deep revealing of oneself." I encourage you to read the full definition for more insight.

While people who are sexually intimate find that sex makes them feel closer, the feeling of closeness obtained *only* through sexuality has a temporary quality. This leads one to believe that after the moment is over maybe those close feelings are gone.

True intimacy in a relationship is one of life's richest rewards: knowing that you can trust one another, that you regard each other's needs as important as your own, and believing that your intimate partner will be there for you, and vice versa. This is why we get so upset when close relationships end. Our secrets are now open and become a source of vulnerability. People become afraid to share themselves again and open up their truest feelings, especially if there were previous betrayals. Fear is one of intimacy's greatest enemies. So great is the fear that most people resign themselves to believing that sexual intimacy is the only intimacy they will ever have.

We all want someone to be our confidant — someone we can tell our feelings to even if they seem ridiculous or unwarranted. We crave someone who won't judge us or hold our secrets against us. (That's why no matter how angry or hurt you are, *never, never* say or do something to your partner that wounds them. While they may be able to forgive you, they will never forget!)

Intimacy grows during life's most wonderful and most horrible events. I remember the day my former husband had to break the news to me that my sister had been killed in an auto accident. I was so glad that he was there for me and that I did not have to be alone with the news. Later, when he went with me to the hospital to see my brother after his accident, I was not alone. Though tragic, incidents like these bring us closer to one another and provide an arena for us to share our innermost hurts, fears, and joys. These events provide a *treasury of memories* with which our lives intertwine, grow, and prosper.

Intimacy demands healthy interdependence. Singles must accept that the need for each other's support in their daily lives is normal. So many singles still feel the need to "keep their options open" or are so afraid that they'll change their mind that relationships may never have a chance to reach the point of rich intimacy. Where there is commitment, intimacy grows. Note: this does not only mean "total" commitment. Varying levels of commitment create varying levels of intimacy. You could make a simple decision (i.e., "Let's date only each other for the summer and see where the relationship goes."). Or, you could decide that your relationship could lead to something more serious. Without some level of commitment, however, singles will spend part of their energy protecting themselves from getting hurt and part preparing for a life that might not include the other partner. Doing this causes a type of separateness that builds walls between two people who might be great for each other.

> _**The bottom line**: having **some** commitment allows a couple to feel safer while creating an intimate bond._

Getting back to sex: Avoid the trap of thinking that sex is the only way to experience intimacy. Try to develop a relationship in which you really get to know each other — not just in the biblical sense. Build that treasury of memories together.

As your intimacy grows so will physical attraction. Enjoy it without "going all the way." Be creative! There are plenty of ways adults can give each other pleasure. You'll find that the discipline of not pursuing sexual intercourse actually heightens your desire for each other and makes the relationship more worthwhile. Then, when *both* of you are ready to create a deeper level of commitment, allow your sexuality to express itself as well. (By the way, three dates is not enough lead time to really decide if you want to get more serious. . . but more on that later).

Create Your Own
Treasury of Intimate Moments

Write them down in a journal so you can remember them always.
Some of my clients share their own.:

"The night I cried for the very first time in my wife's arms created a new opening between us. Crying in her arms, and feeling her acceptance, healed a part of me that I was not even aware needed comfort. I must have hidden these feelings since childhood. After I let my walls down, my sweetheart found the courage to share with me her own hurts, and for the first time I really understood her tears."

"It was when tears welled up in his eyes that I truly realized his capacity for love. Some 20 years after his infant son's death, the remembrances brought him in touch with the loss. I felt honored that he would trust me with his innermost thoughts, even though they were painful. There was a sweet tenderness in my heart for him after that."

"The moments I remember most were not the fireworks but the sound of his voice as he proudly referred to my daughter and me as 'my family. . .'"

"I knew he was afraid to be a father and worried he wouldn't do a good job. . . I knew as soon as she was born and I heard him say, 'Oh wow, oh wow, oh wow!' that he was opening up to a new and very different kind of love."

"I wasn't prepared for the outburst that followed a genuinely touching and almost spiritual love-making. . . until I remembered that Susan said, 'In relationships anything can happen. . . that issues come up for healing.' I was proud that my wife felt safe enough in my arms to reveal that she had been sexually abused as a child. She said that the way I was being with her made her start to believe again that she could let go of the past. We reached a new level in our relationship."

"She was there for me when my mother was in the hospital. I guess she could tell how upset I was even through the nervous jokes I was cracking. She reached over and squeezed my hand and said, 'I'm here for you.'"

"I knew I wanted him in my life forever when he won a stuffed animal at the fair and he gave it away to a little girl who sat there clapping."

"He didn't yell at me when I wrecked the car. It was his car and he loved it, but I found out who he loved more!"

"I know most women think men are devoid of feelings. I used to think that, too, until my guy wrote a song about me. I think men must fall a little harder for us than we think. There are so many male song-writers; they have to feel those feelings in order to write those words."

"I had a really bad day. I don't know how he knew it, but I needed some extra loving. He surprised me with the perfect card and a plaque that had an inspiring message on it. Then I found out that he had this private stash of gifts and cards that he'd collected just to be able to surprise me with from time to time. I've starting doing the same thing now."

You do something to me.

Something that simply mystifies me.

-- Cole Porter
Fifty Million Frenchmen (1929).
You Do Something to Me

ᝰop ᝰwenty-ᝰive ᝰen to ᝰvoid

1. Men who still want women who are only good in two rooms of the house. . . the kitchen and the bedroom.

2. Men who think burping is a talent.

3. Men who wear lots of gold chains around their neck.

4. Men who comb their hair across their bald spot.

5. Men who still wear double-knit polyester and velour shirts.

6. Workaholics or any other "-aholic" (negaholics, alcoholics, etc.). Chocaholics are fine, especially if they'll share.

7. Men who brag about how much beer they can drink before they pass out.

8. Men who have a regular table at the local "Female Revue."

9. Men who call women "little ladies."

10. Men who forget to celebrate Valentine's Day.

11. Men who wear full softball uniforms when they aren't playing.

12. Men who split the bills down the middle. . . and demand every cent.

13. *Men who brag about never wearing a condom.*

14. Men who think women prefer quickies to warm, loving, and caring sex.

15. Men who wear plaid flannel shirts out on a date.

16. Men who try to French kiss you the first time you meet.

17. Men who don't know how to do laundry, or who want you to do it for them.

18. Men who are never available on weekends and holidays.

19. Men who conveniently schedule a fishing trip whenever your mother is coming to visit.

20. Men who conveniently forget their wallet on your first date.

21. Frequent fliers with a woman in every "port."

22. Prevaricators.

23. Men who are prejudiced against children.

24. Men who don't seem to have a home phone number. ("Call me at work, honey, or use my voice mail.")

25. Men who brag about their sperm count.

Chapter Fifteen

On Choosing the Right Mate

Red Flags: The Silent Relationship Killers
Think about your last relationship. When did you begin to notice hints of future dilemmas that caused the breakup? Have you learned to watch and listen for the telltale signs of incompatibility? These signs usually show up early in a relationship but most people ignore them, which is why I've devised the red flag/white flag system.
Red flags are warnings. They are usually subtle things that are said or done. For example: S/he tells a racist joke. You may at first think this an innocent joke but watch out, this could be your first red flag. It becomes a giant STOP sign if the comments and jokes are more frequent and represent his/her true feelings and beliefs. Pay attention! People will always give you clues. Never over-analyze.
Example A: You love fashion and he says, "You always dress so ritzy." This could mean:
A. He appreciates how you dress, or
B. He's separating himself from you, meaning, "I don't dress that way and you do, so maybe we don't fit."
Example B: If you love sausage and she says, "That's fattening." This means:
A. "You really shouldn't eat that." (She supports your health.)
B. Watch out for the tone of voice! This, too, can be a red flag.
BUT! If she says, "Can you come over for dinner? I have some home-made sausage waiting for the right person," this is a *white flag* ¯ a good sign for compatibility (unless you are watching fat grams and cholesterol).
White flags are all the things you enjoy about a person, small or large (e.g., he always opens the door for you; holds your coat; is polite and friendly to strangers, friends, and family; he surprises you with a single flower every once in a while; he has a sense of style; she offers to cook a wonderful meal; unlocks your door when she's warmly inside your car; always takes care of herself, calls to thank you for a wonderful date; treats others with care, etc.).

Red Flags: Things to Watch Out For!

1. Rudeness to anyone.

2. How they act in traffic when they are in a hurry. (Do they call people jerks? We all do sometimes, but is it excessive?)

3. The condition of their shoes. Worn? Not polished? Outdated?

4. Fingernails: clean and neat, or the opposite?

5. Hairstyle: anyone who's had the same style for more than five years could be resistant to changing and growing.

6. Is s/he opinionated or easily led?

7. How they handle themselves in different social situations.

8. Do they run five minutes early or late? (Which one is more compatible for you?) Are you a morning person? Night owl?

9. Little statements where you notice a difference in likes or dislikes.

10. The list could be endless. . . add your own concerns.

Every time you hear, see, or feel something that seems like a little red flag, keep a mental note. These are the symptoms of future problems which, may never develop, but if/when they do, you will be more prepared. However, don't jump to too many conclusions on every little thing. You must have patience and give your partner time. Keep track of white flags, too, which helps to make the system fair. There will always be red and white flags in any type of relationship. But when the red ones outweigh the white, consider not continuing the dating relationship.

It's not good to create and store negative evidence of why you should or shouldn't be with someone. Just *be forewarned*. The classic example of a red flag is: If s/he cheated on her/his last spouse or was still seeing someone else when you two met, history could repeat itself. Or if you notice that s/he gets into rages with family members, when *you* become family you may experience the same thing. (Do you have the skills and patience to deal with this characteristic or not?)

On the other hand, just because someone acts a certain way on a certain day is not enough repetitive evidence to be conclusive about that person. I emphasize the concept of **repetition.**

In analyzing red/white flags, ask yourself these questions: What are your long term goals? Do those of your potential mate's coincide? How far off are they? Compatibility does not mean that you think and do all things alike. For some people that would be too boring.

Use good "business sense" when choosing a partner. A successful business manager does not hire people with the same type of personality to do the different jobs that need to be done. We need people with different strengths and weaknesses to complement who we are, what we do, and how we operate in life.

Reflect on this question: "If we were sitting in a room with all of your ex-significant others, what would they say about you — positively and negatively?" Wouldn't it be nice to know the answer to this question of anyone you date?

Once we end a relationship or recognize its problems, we can more easily put together the puzzle pieces of how we got there. Hindsight gives us 20/20 vision to see the red flags. *But, if you begin now to notice them and take mental inventory when they occur, you'll be protecting yourself.* You won't be as mystified, victimized, or shocked when the "big ones" occur. The straws that seem to break the camel's back will be noticeable one by one.

White flags keep the relationship together and happy, but red ones keep us growing and dealing with issues before they become unmanageable. If someone says something to you tomorrow and a light goes off in your head —"Uh-oh, potential toxic waste! Red flag! Red flag!" — just acknowledge its existence, but do not dwell on it. It may just be an area where you don't share the same opinions or likes/dislikes. But, if the issue seems more serious to you, you may need to discuss it, or wait and watch what develops.

Someone I was dating for about a month said: "I hate downtown. I never like going there." I, on the other hand, love going downtown and frequently attend benefits, business meetings, etc. His statement was a red flag which informed me that this was a hint of a future conflict area. For example: Suppose I really wanted to attend a certain event downtown, such as a play or concert, but his only reason for not going was because he just didn't like downtown. I would then have three choices: compromise, go alone, or not go at all.

If he says, "I'm just a country boy," take this as a warning. He means, "We might not work out if you don't want to make trekking around in the mud a priority, and don't ask me to do too many citified activities on dates."

When someone says, "I want to get to know the real you," don't you wonder who they think you were being before? Sometimes it seems as if people who are happy-go-lucky with an upbeat attitude aren't taken at face value. Instead, others are waiting for the inevitable negative side to pop out. If someone says this or something like it to you, assume that they just wants to get to know you more thoroughly and in different situations.

You must choose what you can live with. If, however, you know that you would not want to date anyone who has opinions and limitations, even as seemingly inconsequential as these, it may be better to stop the relationship now. White flags balance red flags. But, if the red flags out-number the white, it would be much better to end the relationship early on before anything more serious develops.

Intimacy Turning Points

Most relationships end after the first date; even more end after the third. If a dating relationship lasts longer than three months, it has a better chance of making it. The next crucial turning points are at six months, nine months, one year, and a year and a half. If commitment does not happen by the two-year mark, you might be wasting your time in the relationship. After 90 days, intimacy can occur on a safer level. By this time, you've both seen each other with 5 o'clock shadow, no makeup, etc. and you haven't been scared away.

If you look hard enough and long enough for something right or wrong, you'll find evidence. Be forewarned, but stay away from being too analytical.

> **Two persons cannot long be friends if they cannot forgive each other's little failings.**
>
> *-- Jean de la Fontaine*

Prepare for Your Relationship's Success
By Eliminating These Red Flags

25 Relationship Killers
(Or, How to Prevent Love From Happening in Your Life)

1. Stay the way you are and make no improvements.

2. Be negative or talk negatively.

3. Sweep things under the carpet, don't rock the boat, take the easy way out.

4. Pick wrong people to love.

5. Use your partner for sexual fix.

6. Don't let go of past relationships.

7. Play traditional roles.

8. Control or hide feelings.

9. Be a know-it-all.

10. Hold on to ego (your need to be right).

11. Stifle partner's freedom of expression.

12. Use income to control.

13. Punish honest communication.

14. Put career or anything before your love relationship.

15. Put sex before love.

16. Limit communication.

17. Behavior addictions: alcohol, drugs, smoking, TV, sports, gambling, 1-900 sex numbers, shopping, work, overeating.

18. Let fear of closeness and vulnerability create endless excuses for not having a relationship or not getting closer with your current partner.

19. Don't live life to the fullest.

20. Have kids too soon.

21. Allow past issues with parents/past relationships to surface with and poison potential mates.

22. Don't complete or heal from past relationships.

23. Act too needy or desperate.

24. CO-dependency.

25. Jealousy.

We have all been guilty of some of these "Relationship Killers" at some point in our life. Prevent them from ruining your soulmating potential by recognizing when the behaviors surface. Spend less time being stuck in them and more time learning and growing. It's like noticing that there is spinach between your teeth: you can agonize over its being there, or you can do something about it.

Much of our self-talk is abusive. In fact, if we played your self- talk over a loud speaker and imagined it was a parent saying it to a child, we *would* call it abuse. Be committed to getting unstuck quickly and as painlessly as possible.

**Never, *never*, *NEVER*
say something hurtful
or vengeful
to your partner.
S/he may forgive you,
but forget about the forgetting!**

**Treasure the love you receive above all.
It will survive long after your gold
and good health have vanished.**

-- *Og Mandino*

ᗧop ᗴeventeen ᗯomen to ᗩvoid

1. The eternal critic.

2. Women who wear curlers in their hair to bed or in public.

3. Women who spend too much time getting ready to go out to the supermarket.

4. Women who want you to explain the punch line of a "blonde" joke.

5. Women who believe that sex is only for procreation.

6. Women who don't know how to balance a checking account.

7. Women who think shopping is a career and credit cards are time cards.

8. Women who pretend they can't change light bulbs or use screwdrivers.

9. Women who judge your worth by the thickness of your wallet.

10. Women whose biological clocks are ticking so loud that once a month they rent the movie "Three Men and a Baby."

11. Women who treat you like a child.

12. Women who monitor your food intake.

13. Women who carry PMS excuse cards.

14. Women who are more worried about their fingernails breaking than the dent they put in your car.

15. Women who drive from the passenger seat.

16. Women who shriek.

17. Women who whine.

Chapter Sixteen

Compatibility and Physical Chemistry

I could fall in love every day if I wanted to. I meet wonderful men all the time. They come in so many different sizes and packages, and most women don't know where to find the good ones. A lot of people don't even believe that anyone wonderful really exists. Whether you're male or female, if you've ever been hurt in a relationship, you've probably felt that way at some time in your life.

Any one of us could fall for someone, but that does not mean that they would be right for us long-term. Most people ignore the red flags at the beginning of a relationship because they feel "chemistry." Others throw away a perfectly good man or woman just because they lack the feelings of "chemistry" and "attraction." The truth is that sometimes it takes more than one date or phone call to create chemistry. Sometimes it takes more than a month. So if someone has very pleasing qualities but fails to inspire "chemistry," give it some more time and read up on Attraction Strategies. (Attraction Strategies create "chemistry"; see Chapter Twelve.)

Sometimes women abandon a potential relationship because the guy is so "nice," meaning he doesn't pressure her by the third date with sexual advances. If you're not at least getting hugs and kisses (semi-formal ones) by the third date, assume your guy is shy. The "nice," respectful guy who doesn't want to rush the situation wants some indication from the female on how fast to proceed. Unfortunately, this causes him to get the label "NGB" (NICE GUY, BUT. . .). If there isn't some sort of attempt towards more intimacy (I stress *attempt*), the woman may feel that her guy isn't really interested in her.

Let me define "the attempt": usually a two-second kiss or a hug at the end of the first or second date, depending on how well things go. A longer more passionate kiss (five seconds) at the end of the first date will be interpreted by the woman as an indication that you're "only interested in sex." This will lower your chances of long-term success.

Ladies, help the guys out. If you are interested in him and you notice he's a little uncomfortable when he walks you to the door or car, try saying in a fun tone of voice, with a smile, "This is the part where the boy kisses the girl." I have found it works quite well. Men secretly fear the old slap in the face, even though women don't (usually) do that anymore.

Another tip, ladies: If you want him to open your car door for you — or any door — remain seated or pause before the door until he can get there. Believe me, he will appreciate knowing what you want. Because some women resent men who open doors, etc., it can be very confusing for the opposite sex.

First date protocol includes a quick squeeze of the hand whenever appropriate. This can be done by either sex. The proper progression of intimacy begins with eye to body contact, then eye to eye, voice to voice, hand to hand touching, hand to shoulder, (all of this is appropriate in the beginning) face to face (i.e. kissing, gazing into each others eyes, hugging) hand to head (gently touching your partners' face, head or hair). The next bonding steps get progressively more sexual in nature, but that's for another book. All of the above elements help create "chemistry." However, chemistry alone is not enough. Determine your attraction strategy and take a strong look at compatibility or you could end up in an unhappy situation three months to one year down the road.

Begin working on determining compatibility now. Make a list of ten qualities you would want in a partner (for example, likes children, outgoing, responsible, sexy, helpful, spiritual, etc.):

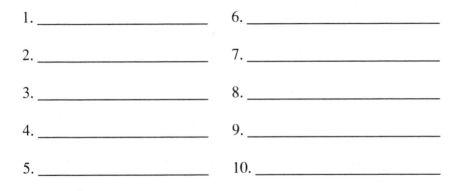

1. _____   6. _____

2. _____   7. _____

3. _____   8. _____

4. _____   9. _____

5. _____   10. _____

Continue with the next section for an in-depth view of compatibility factors.

**The heart has its reasons
which reason knows nothing of.**

-- Blaise Pascal
Pensées (1670), no. 2

**A woman without a man cannot meet a
man, any man, of any age, without thinking,
even if it's for a half-second,
"Perhaps this is 'THE MAN."**

-- Doris Lessing
The Golden Notebook **(1962). Free Women, 5**

Compatibility Factors

Many people want to know:

How will I recognize "the one"?

First, believe that there are lots of wonderful choices for you out there and practice "knowing" that someone could be "the one." Second, practice, practice, practice. In the beginning of a relationship, look for compatibility factors, notice how you feel, and watch out for red flags. Let time be your best friend and don't rush in too fast, no matter how tempting it is.

People frequently end up in relationships that I call "intermediate": they **further your growth and understanding of love at this point in your life.** When you've both completed these lessons, you may realize that he or she is not "the one." You were both instrumental for each other to heal a certain aspect of your past , but when the healing occurs, it will be time to say this Four-Letter-Word:

N-E-X-T!

An "intermediate" relationship occurs most often with people who have just ended a painful relationship. Do not allow the past to stop you from caring again. The intermediate relationship can support you in getting back on that proverbial horse again. Involve yourself with someone better and safer than the last person/people you chose. Once you learn what this relationship has to offer, recognize that, while this person is a super person, s/he may not be someone that you could remain compatible with in the long term. Allow yourself to have as many "intermediate relationships" as you need. Each one will teach you and bring you closer to "the one."

Right now, as you read this,
someone out there is sitting around,
scratching their head, and waiting for YOU
to show up in their life!

To prevent wasting time with people who are *not your type*, begin using what you have learned about red flags — the little tell-tale signs that warn you of a potentially toxic relationship. Combine that with what you have learned about "true intimacy," then remember to avoid the pitfalls of thinking that physical chemistry really "means" something. Now you are ready to add the element of:

P-E-P-S-I Compatibility Factors

P = PHYSICAL COMPATIBILITY
E = EMOTIONAL
P = PROSPERITY (or financial compatibility)
S = SPIRITUAL
I = INTELLECTUAL COMPATIBILITY

No disguise can long conceal love
where it is, nor feign it, where it is not.

-- *La Rochefoucauld*

With each category of the PEPSI Factors, list the top five qualities that are most important for you in a potential mate. Only you can decide what qualities you really can't live without. See the chart on the next page for a few examples.

Physical	Emotional	Prosperity	Spiritual	Intellectual
Tall/short	Open/ closed	Has a job	Atheist	Education
Blond or brunette	Overt or covert	Owns a home	Christian	Follower or leader
Attractive or average	Bubbly or reserved	Generous	Catholic	Reader or non-reader
Exercises	Depend- ent	Thrifty	Jewish	Etiquette
Race	Free spirit	Middle- class	Orthodox	Analytical
Ethnic backgroun d	Caring or matter of fact	Upper class	Born- again	Level of sophistic- ation
Thin/aver- age build	Quiet or talkative	White or blue collar	Attends religious services	Casual
Well dressed or average	Balanced	Income level	Mutual beliefs	Savvy

Now, arrange the factors in order of highest importance. Use the form found at the end of this section for prioritizing the importance of each item. Have your friends try this and see how different they are.

**It is easier to resist at the beginning
than at the end.**

**-- *Leonardo da Vinci*
The Notebooks (1508-1518), vol. I, ch. 2I**

> **If you press me to say why I loved him, I can say no more than it was because he was he and I was I.**
>
> **-- *Michel de Montaigne* Essays, bk. I (1580), ch. 28**

To Discover Other C-Factors,
Ask Great Compatibility Questions

Some examples:

1. What do we have in common in each P-E-P-S-I category?

2. If you only had 30 days to live, how would you spend them? Assume that you could do anything you wanted, and that you had all the money and power you needed. (Answers to this question will help you understand what makes this person tick and will give you clues as to what they value the most.)

3. What would your ex say was the reason for your breakup? (Pay close attention, because truth is found on both sides. Answers may give you a clue as to what might be in store for you. For example: The former spouse may say, "He always helped the neighbors fix everything before he would fix anything around here. It was as if everyone else came first." Take this hint very literally, and be prepared to have this occur in your life together, too. If this type of behavior seems like something you could not deal with in the long run. . . RUN in the opposite direction. A former spouse might also tell you such things as, "When she drinks, she gets violent." Don't delude yourself into thinking it will be any different with you. Remember: it could take up to three years to change major negative behaviors.)

4. Describe your ideal lifestyle/house/car and why you want things this way.

5. In ten years, where do you think you'll be living? What will you have accomplished? What will your life be like?

Compatibility Prioritizing Form Instructions

Select any one P-E-P-S-I idea, question or category and try the exercises below. You will become more adept at choosing your next ("the ONE") or will learn more about your current significant other.

Use the form on the next page to define the qualities you are looking for in P-E-P-S-I. Take one category, such as physical qualities, and list the ten wishes that you have in this area Then use the form to discover what your true priorities are. Sometimes you will be surprised. One man thought that physical attractiveness and having a good build would be high on his list. After completing the compatibility form, however, he was surprised to find that a woman's ability to cook and share his enjoyment of food were more important.

As you use the form your priorities will become clearer to you in each of the five areas: physical, emotional, prosperity, spirituality, and intellectual. You may even wish to add the category of Sensuality.

Instructions

1. Decide which P-E-P-S-I category you will use. Or begin with a general list of ten items which could include the top ten qualities you would want in a mate, etc.

2. List your qualities, in any order, in the blanks to the left of the grid (under Section A).

3. Compare each quality for importance using the grid under Section B (compare item 1 to item 2, then 1 to 3, etc.).

    Hint: See the "fractions" to the right of each quality? 1/2 means "compare #1 to #2," 1/3 means "compare #1 to #3," etc.

4. For each "fraction," circle the *number* of the quality that feels more important. *Note: Don't think too hard. Don't rationalize. Use your first instinct.*

5. When you have compared each quality and completed the form, add the number of 1's you circled, and write the total in the right-hand column under Section C, then add up the number of 2's, 3's, etc., for each quality, and write the totals in Section C. **Note:** After the 1's, you must add horizontally and vertically to get an accurate total.

6. When you have completed Section C, you may see that you have some "tie" votes. Use the blanks under Section D, "Ties," to more easily compare these. Add one half a point to the quality you value most. Now you're ready to complete and prioritize your list!

7. Using the ratings from Section C, list your qualities in order of importance in Section E.

    Tip for Instructions 3 & 4: When my daughter was five she had a method for choosing pies at the bakery. She called it the Eenie-Meenie-Miney-Moe Method. Try it: it might work for you, too! She just pointed back and forth to each pie and said, "Eenie-Meenie-Miney-Moe; catch the baby by the toe; if he hollers let him go. Eenie-Meenie-Miney-Moe!" If it wasn't what she really wanted, she'd chant: "My mother says to pick the very best one and you are it!" Whichever pie she was pointing to when she said the word "it" was the winner. You probably played this game, too, once upon a time!

    One day I noticed that if she did not like the results, she would simply go through the jingle again and again until she got the "right answer." *Of course, she already knew unconsciously what she really wanted but hadn't given herself the permission and freedom to just decide!* **Many of us are like that, too. So, go with your first hunch -OR- use the Eenie-Meenie-Miney-Moe jingle.**

Use Section D for Ties

What should you do if 2 or 3 qualities have the same number of points? Let's say Caring, Fun, and Adventurous all received 3 points.

1. Compare Caring to Fun. Which one is more meaningful to you? Caring? Give it 1/4 point and add it to the final rank area in Section C.

2. Now, compare Caring to Adventurous. Caring wins again? Give it another 1/4 point. Now, Caring has a total of 3 1/2 points.

3. Finally, compare Fun to Adventurous, If fun is more important, give it 1/4 point.

4. Final Tally:
   Caring = 3 1/2 pts.
   Fun = 3 1/4 pts.
   Adventurous = 3 pts.
   Your 3-way tie is now broken!

When coaching a client, I usually ask them to use this form in three different ways.
1. List the top ten qualities you desire in a best friend.
2. List the top ten qualities you would want in a boss.
3. List the top ten qualities in the "perfect" mate.

Compare the lists, noticing similarities and differences. Wouldn't you like your mate to be your best friend? Sometimes your mate will act like your boss, and vice versa. What qualities would you want your mate to exhibit if s/he were the one in authority? Filling out the form in the above suggested ways will provide further clarity in these overlapping areas.

Compatibility Prioritizing Form

WARNING! This form is one of the most powerful components of this entire book. Take the time NOW to fill it out and it will allow you to create an irresistible relationship, as well as easily pass up the "wrong" type for you. Below is a sample list. It may give you ideas when you fill yours out!

A: List the top ten qualities you want in a mate or career (not in order).

I	A.	I	B.	I	C.	I	D. Extra Pts.

1. *open minded*   > 1's _8_   ___

2. *health oriented* (1)2   > 2's _5_   ___

3. *accepts child* (1)3 2(3)   > 3's _7_   ¼=7¼

4. *prosperity* > (1)4 2(4)(3)4   > 4's _5_   ¼=5¼

5. *spiritual* > (1)5 2(5) 3(5) 4(5)   > 5's _7_   ___

6. *adventurous* > (1)6 (2)6 (3)6 (4)6 (5)6   > 6's _0_   ___

7. *takes seminars* (1)7 (2)7 (3)7 (4)7 (5)7 6(7)   > 7's _2_   ___

8. *dresses well* > (1)8 (2)8 (3)8 4(8)(5)8 6(8) 7(8) > 8's _4_   ___

9. *sensual* > (1)9 (2)9 (3)9 (4)9 (5)9 6(9)(7)9 (8)9 > 9's _1_   ___

10. *contributes* > 1(10)(2)10 (3)10 (4)10 5(10) 6(10) 7(10) 8(10) 9(10)
    to humanity   > 10's _6_   ___

Compare quality 1 to quality 2, and circle the one which is more important. (When adding up the points, remember to count the circled numbers *horizontally and vertically*).

D. Tie Breaker

accepts child vs. *spiritual* = *accepts child*
The winner receives 1/4 pt.

prosperity vs. *health oriented* = *prosperity*
The winner receives 1/4 pt.

_____ vs. _____ = _____
The winner receives 1/4 pt.

E. Final Order

1. *open minded*   95 %

2. *accepts child*   100 %

3. *spiritual*   75 %

4. *contributes to humanity*   85 %

5. *prosperity*   80 %

6. *health oriented*   90 %

7. *dresses well*   80 %

8. *takes seminars*   100 %

9. *sensual*   90 %

10. *adventurous*   90 %

If you want to take the use of this form even further, rate your potential mate on a percentage scale of 1-100%, then ask your mate to rate you. You may be pleasantly surprised! Let's say that the #1 quality you want in a mate is "open-mindedness."

How open minded is s/he? If you can't at least give your partner an 80%, then you may have some serious compatibility challenges. Look at the rest of the qualities in the same manner. Even if "open-minded" were #8 in priority, remember that it made your top ten list and is still very important.

One of my clients realized that her fiancé fell into the 80-100% category in eight out of ten qualities but rated a 20% in two categories: taking care of his health and spirituality. Needless to say, all of their conflicts centered around eating, exercise, and religion. Since meals are daily events, this created conflict daily. They eventually called off the engagement. Her new fiancé takes seminars with her, goes to church, likes to exercise, and watches what he eats. Their lifestyles are much more compatible. *If she hadn't been willing to let go of a good guy to find a more compatible guy, they'd still be making each other miserable.*

Now it's Your Turn

Compatibility (Mate Selection) Form

A: List the top ten qualities you want in a mate or career (not in order).

I A.	I B.	I C.	I D. Extra Pts.
1._____>		> 1's____	____
2._____> 1/2		> 2's____	____
3._____> 1/3 2/3		> 3's____	____
4._____> 1/4 2/4 3/4		> 4's____	____
5._____> 1/5 2/5 3/5 4/5		> 5's____	____
6._____> 1/6 2/6 3/6 4/6 5/6		> 6's____	____
7._____> 1/7 2/7 3/7 4/7 5/7 6/7		> 7's____	____
8._____> 1/8 2/8 3/8 4/8 5/8 6/8 7/8		> 8's____	____
9._____> 1/9 2/9 3/9 4/9 5/9 6/9 7/9 8/9	> 9's____	____
10._____> 1/10 2/10 3/10 4/10 5/10 6/10 7/10 8/10 9/10			
		> 10's____	____

Compare quality 1 to quality 2, and circle the one which is more important. (When adding up the points, remember to count the circled numbers *horizontally and vertically*).

D. Tie Breaker

_____ vs. _____ = _____
    The winner receives 1/4 pt.

_____ vs. _____ = _____
    The winner receives 1/4 pt.

_____ vs. _____ = _____
    The winner receives 1/4 pt.

E. Final Order

1. _____ _____%

2. _____ _____%

3. _____ _____%

4. _____ _____%

5. _____ _____%

6. _____ _____%

7. _____ _____%

8. _____ _____%

9. _____ _____%

10. _____ _____%

Re-use this form as your priorities change or if you realize that you forgot to include a quality. This form is reprinted from the book "Dating ♥ Mating ♥ Relating" Call 1-800-COMPATIBLE (1-800-266-7284) to order your own copy.

Top Eleven Reasons to Get Married & Stay Married

1. Taxes!

2. Children.

3. Having someone to take out the garbage!

4. Frequent and unlimited sex.

5. To stop dating.

6. Having someone to help with car repairs and laundry.

7. Having someone to grow old and decrepit with.

8. Having someone to "do life" with.

9. No more TV dinners.

10. Warming up cold feet.

11. Having someone to count on when life is not fair.

The first 90 days of a relationship, a.k.a. the "stupid period" — you stop seeing your friends, doing your laundry and only fantasize about your new partner. Day 91 is a turning point. You realize they're imperfect like you. This is the time to let go or commit to go all the way in developing total trust.

— Susan Bradley

Closing The Deal: Getting to the Altar

Signs that you are ready to make a deeper commitment:

1. You have already:
   - ✓ Completed Audio/Visual/Kinetic Compatibility Questions.
   - ✓ Compared lifestyles.
   - ✓ Completed the *Companion Guide.*
   - ✓ Completed P-E-P-S-I Compatibility Factors.
   - ✓ Completed the Compatibility Prioritizing Form.
   - ✓ Rated your prospective mate based on qualities you have experienced and not just future potential.

2. You trust this person and do not want him/her to change.

3. You want to learn and grow with this person.

4. You have not only been in love with this person, but also love him or her.

5. You feel pangs of emptiness or a longing when you are separated.

6. You feel a general feeling of wellness and comfort together.

7. You are able to share this book and other relationship books with your partner.

8. You are able to move through any upsets in hours rather than days.

9. You have met each other's family, including any children.

10. You have discussed the major issues (children, work, where to live, finances, who's paying for what, how to deal with parents, etc.) without strangling each other.

Signs that your partner is
checking you out for marriage:

Men, either consciously or unconsciously, start testing you. They will ask questions such as how many children you want or what you would do if your husband ever lost his job. These questions will come at different times and be woven into conversation so that their importance is not readily noticeable. However, they *are* important.

Men sometimes start acting out to see if you try to change them. They will do little things to irritate you just to see how you react. The best reaction is loving acceptance while making it clear what kind of behavior works for you and what does not. No lectures. Be his loving partner, not his mother.

Women are more verbal than men about their intentions for the relationship, especially when they want to know what *your* intentions are. Marriage-oriented questions are sure to come up after you've spent four seasons together and maybe before. This is what many women do: Ask you lots of questions regarding children and/or living arrangements (What color couch do you like? When you settle down, how often will you want to go out with your buddies? How many children do you want?) When they see babies, they point them out to you. They talk about other friends' engagements and weddings. Look for these hints.

I interviewed hundreds of men and women with this question: How and when did you know that your wife/husband was the one for you?

Men were ten times more likely to say they knew that she was the one at first sighting or after a few dates. Women generally took a lot longer (minimum time 2 months) although some said they knew the moment they met.

"There was this window of opportunity that only happens a few times in your life. I was on the runway waiting to leave and I looked up at her and said, "What are you doing with the rest of your life? Will you marry me?"

-- A Well-Known Editor

"I knew the first time I met her. In fact, I went home and told my roommate and he said I was crazy. We've been married 15 years. I asked her when she was crawling out my dorm window in college. She of course said, "Yes."
   -- Paul K.

He said: "I knew by the second date that she was the one." She said: "I knew eight weeks after we met." He said: "It was just a feeling. I can't explain it, but I knew."
   -- John and Laurie

"It was a very tumultuous year. A lot had happened. When I met Naomi I felt a stirring in my heart, a feeling of light and aliveness that I hadn't known for a long time. That's how I knew."
   -- Joe Ezsterhas (screenwriter of "Basic Instinct" and "Flash Dance")

It sort of just happened. . . we'd been dating for two years and I sat down one night and said I guess I should marry her and we've been together 35 years.
   -- Peg and Jack, astrologers

Many men discover a new person lurking within when they fall in love. They report to me, "I swore I would never act this way. . . Oh well!" Many times it's only when men have perceived a loss. Notice I say *perceived* a loss — their lady goes away on a business trip, visits her family out of town, or takes a vacation, and the sense of loss that they feel makes them realize that they want this woman in their life for a long time.
   Often a break-up over some issue results in the realization that, "I just can't live without my partner!" Sometimes, this revelation comes too late. Most men wait too long to give women the hint that they really care for them. By that time, the woman unconsciously gets the message that there's no hope, and moves on.

Some men, who never knew they were writers, find themselves more able to express themselves once they realize how much they are in love. The following letter was written by an auto mechanic who swears he has never written anything in his lifetime before falling in love with Anna:

Dear Anna,

They say you know when that special person comes into your life. I realized it was you one Wednesday night in October when we were out at dinner. I picked you up right after work and it was only our seventh date. I will always remember that time. While walking back to the table, looking at your smile. . . I knew you were the one for me. The more we dated the more I was sure of my feelings.

One night when things were not going well, being with you was all I needed. Sitting on the couch, holding you, even though we did not talk. . . being in my arms was enough. The emotion that came over me when I was holding you was more than you could ever understand. I remember looking at you and telling you "Thanks." Your reply was, "I didn't do anything." But, you did, without knowing it.

The caring that you showed me along with your trust is something that I have not found in anyone else. These qualities and many others that come to you so naturally mean so much to me. I think that you show and give them without knowing.

The dinners we had, the shows we've seen, the rides we took — I enjoyed them all. And I was looking forward to seeing more plays with you. If only I could have conveyed to you my feelings before it was too late. If I could change one thing I would have told you more often just how I felt.

I did not realize it, but people told me that they knew without my saying anything just what I was feeling. Different people on different occasions told me that they could tell by the tone of my voice that I had serious feelings for you. While talking to my cousin one night, she told her husband that just by listening to me talk, she knew that a special person had come into my life. When I asked her how she knew, she said, "It was reflected in your voice whenever you talked about her."

I hope it is not too late to let you know that I still feel this way about you. What I would like to do, if possible is just put these last few months behind us and start again. I just wish I could hold you in my arms once again.

You will always be in my heart,

Dan

Dan had waited too long to tell Anna how he felt and she had already moved on to date someone new, thinking that there was no hope for this particular relationship. Ladies, we need to support our men in expressing their true feelings to us. Gentlemen: the letter speaks for itself. Like oxygen, only after missing Anna in his life did Dan realize how much he really loved her.

For Women Only

If I could convince you of only one thing with this book, it would be to open up your hearts again and realize that men are incredible, delectable creatures who truly want to be there for you, support you, shelter you, please you, and heal you. More men desire permanent arrangements than women, for a variety of reasons. *Men aren't bad by nature. They are guilty of speaking/thinking in testosterone, but that doesn't make them bad—just different in expressing who they are.* If they've become callous or seem self-serving, remember that wounds of rejection make them put on this front or wall of protection. They are responsible for healing themselves, but the walls can be melted once you understand how.

Our female walls can be melted, too, once we heal our past wounds and learn to forgive. Read *The Men We Never Knew*, by Daphne Rose Kingma and *To Be a Man*, by Daniel Kaufman and you'll begin to understand more.

I encourage you to begin viewing the men in your life as healers. Allow them to contribute to your life. Start to understand and accept their testosterone ways. Look for them to begin the journey into love. You're probably asking yourself, "Healers? What do you mean? Men as healers?" When you are upset about something that has happened in your life and a man puts his arm around you and says, "We'll get through this together. I'm here for you always and *in* all ways," and as he continues to hold you, you can hear his heart beating, the room is silent, and you feel at peace, then you'll begin to experience the healing.

When men are given opportunities to give to you, love you in their own way and grow with you, the healing begins. At a moment when you are so angry at him that you don't know whether to run out the door and never come back; or when you've said awful things to him and he stays and holds you gently, even though you resist and continue to throw darts, you'll feel the healing, the security of knowing that your man isn't going to run at the first sign of trouble.

I tell men to watch out for this scenario: Every woman at some point in a relationship will tell a man to leave, to get out of her life, though she secretly hopes that he'll come after her and say "No don't go. . . I love you." The guy needs to hold her close with warm, loving arms. Even if "the cat keeps kicking and scratching," hold her close, gently and lovingly, until you hear her sigh and relax. . . because you have proven your love for her. This is where the men get to show their inner strength.

Healing will also occur by simply listening. . . and listening and listening. No matter what she says, be absolutely present to her, conscious of what she's saying and feeling, even if you don't totally understand it, even if it doesn't make any sense, even if it hurts. Be prepared to prove that you've listened by quoting what she said.

In this way men heal their women. However, if the woman gets a sense that her guy is not 100% there mentally and emotionally, she'll start repeating herself and will go on and on about her upset. Do yourself a favor: *listen the first time, even if it seems like it would be easier to enlist in the army and go directly to the forefront of battle.* When a woman feels heard and she's talked it all out, she will find solutions and healing. I will repeat this again: *she will be healed and nurtured and you can take the credit.*

Watch out, though, she may calm down for a few minutes, making you think it's over. . . but it may not be. Never discount how important the issue is to her. She may think of something else that will set her off temporarily and she'll seem upset again. Don't worry, it will be for a much shorter interval. Expect this to happen several times before she's gotten it out of her system. Be prepared to ask questions like: "How did that make you feel?" Tell her: "I'm so sorry that affected you that way. Tell me more. What are you going to do about it?" (Do not offer any solutions unless she specifically asks.)

Sometimes the smallest things can hurt and wound your woman. Though something may seem trivial to you, perhaps even imaginary, it's real to her, and important. . . just like the little things in the treasury of memories that you share. It's usually those little moments that you remember forever.

**If you've gotten past all of the above
you may be ready to deal with this:**

The Marriage Proposal

If there is only one thing you remember from this book, let it be this: **make the proposal a beautiful memory. It *must* be romantic.** Even if you've talked about getting married before a formal proposal, plan a special dinner, a surprise, a way of publicly announcing your love for her. It may seem corny, but it's still very touching to honor a woman by giving her a ring in some clever way, watching her face, and then getting on your knees (yes, I said, "on your knees"), and asking her to join you in marriage. . . asking her to marry you. . . asking her if she will spend the rest of her life with you. *All of this is more important than you could ever believe.*

Many men buy a ring and they are so excited that the ring seems to burn a hole in their pocket, and then they end up blurting out the question late at night when she comes home from work or at some other ordinary moment. Make the experience memorable for both of you, and especially for her. All of her friends will ask her how you proposed. Every time she relates the story, you want her to feel that moment again in her heart. Each time she retells the experience she will feel the good feelings again, and it will cement your bond together.

Don't be proud; ask friends to help you plan it. Do it publicly, do it on a plane, call a radio station and ask them to help you propose to your sweetheart — there are so many ways to do it. Make a giant card (4 ft. x 6 ft.) and put it in her front yard. Be creative; you'll be rewarded many times over.

For Men Only

If you do not take the time to make the proposal a special memory, this could happen to you: When her friends and family ask her how you proposed, you don't want her to admit to herself and to others how disappointing it was. For example: Julie: "Well, he just asked me on the way to the movies. I was hoping for something a bit more special. People expect me to come up with some romantic way, and I do wish he had planned it more. I'm happy to be married to him, don't get me wrong."

Julie is missing out on that proud feeling. Your fiancée will also feel apologetic and a little sad every time she has to tell it that way if she does not have a romantic story to tell. If you love her, spare her those negative feelings. Make it special. . . If you can't afford a diamond, buy another type of ring to propose with and let her know that you'd like to pick out a ring together at a later date. This will allow her to participate in the experience. (If you have already proposed, buy her another ring and re-propose as a surprise. Tell her you would marry her all over again.)

Suggestion: Buy a beautiful cocktail ring while you are on vacation together. Even one that costs $200 would work. You can always buy a diamond solitaire another time.

Vacations are one of the best times to propose. Christmas, Valentine's Day and New Year's Eve are popular as well. Create some fireworks on July 4th. . . Do it on a boat. . . at the top of the Statue of Liberty. . . do it on stage, do it on top of a mountain, do it in a parasail. . .

Tip: Don't just pop the question if you've never told her that you love her. Saying you love her comes first, hinting at marriage next, and then proposing. Giving her a ring and proposing the first time you express the depth of your feelings for her is too risky. It does not allow you time to make sure that the feelings are mutual. Feel out the situation ahead of time by hinting that you are interested in a more permanent relationship.

Even if you do the preliminary checking out, you'll still feel nervous, excited anticipation just before the proposal itself.

If a woman only remembers you for the proposal you gave her, and it was a great experience, even if you ended up in divorce at some point. . . it's a good story for the children, grandchildren, and one positive memory that sticks.

When I first met Norman, he held my hand a fraction of an instance longer than he needed to. I said "This is going to be interesting." It took him two years to persuade me to marry him.

-- *Mrs. Ruth Stafford Peale*, Wife of Dr. Norman Vincent Peale

---

. . .the essential ingredients for a relationship are affection and commitment. . . If it is romance that we seek, it is romance that we shall have, but not commitment and not relationship.

-- *Roberta Johnson*

Marriage is not a static state between two unchanging people. Marriage is a psychological and spiritual journey that begins in the ecstasy of attraction, meanders through a rocky stretch of self discovery, and culminates in the creation of an intimate, joyful, lifelong union.

-- *Harville Hendrix*

Check out our Web site:

http://www.cupidnet.com/cupid/loveuniv/index.html
or
http://www.lovingu.com/lovingu
or
E-mail address: LovingUniv@aol.com

Relating

The path to peaceful and joyful

"REALationships"

begins with the decision to hone your day-to-day

relating skills. Try treating any REALationship

like a garden. First, prepare the foundation

with loose fertile soil, removing any weeds and

large rocks (your emotional baggage), plant

the seeds (date), fertilize (add some romance),

water (communicate daily), prune (watch your

boundaries), weed (eliminate unhealthy behaviors

and habits), and enjoy the growth.

> Know, my love, that I should like to call you a
> thief, because you have stolen my heart.
>
> -- *Margaret of Nassau*

> Friendship is the marriage of the soul.
>
> -- *Voltaire*

> I was at a party feeling very shy because there
> were a lot of celebrities around and I was sitting
> in a corner alone. A very beautiful young man
> came up to me and offered me some salted peanuts
> and he said: "I wish they were emeralds," as
> he handed me the peanuts and that was the
> end of my heart. I never got it back.
>
> -- *Helen Hayes*

Chapter Seventeen
Relating: The Skills That Keep it Going!

Growing a Relationship

Communicating before the little things become major issues takes practice. But doing so creates more ease, dignity, and balance in growing a friendship or relationship. A couple of points to keep in mind:

Always use "I" statements; such as, "I feel uncomfortable when you talk about your last boyfriend, kiss me in public," etc. "I prefer to talk on the phone earlier in the evening."

Never use "YOU" statements. They make people feel defensive and put down; e.g., "You make me angry when you call me too late; talk about your last boyfriend," etc.

If you communicate a difference with someone and s/he reacts badly, discount your emotions, or tell you you're wrong for explaining your needs and wants, perhaps this isn't the right relationship for you. You can decide to call it quits and be thankful it didn't go any further. Don't be afraid to do that, if necessary.

Too many people feel that "a relationship should just happen." A garden could just happen, too — with weeds, bugs, and pests. How fruitful a relationship is depends on two people knowing when to "fertilize, weed, and prune anything unwanted, and when to enjoy the harvest." Poor attention can cause "disease," that feeling of uneasiness in a relationship: neglect, not getting enough attention (for which cards, calls, flowers, candlelight dinners, surprises — and not just on Valentine's Day or Sweetest Day — could be cures). Or the opposite can occur: too much attention (over-watering) in calling too much, not giving that person much needed alone-time, etc., can cause disease also.

> **Living the past is a dull and lonely business; looking back strains the neck muscles and causes you to bump into people not going your way.**
>
> *-- Ferber*

Growing a Relationship

(Follow directions on
    packet.)

- **Prepare the ground.** Be
  ready for a relationship.
  Eliminate negative
  beliefs/baggage, such as
  your thoughts and feelings
  about ex-significant others.

- **Plant the seeds.** Date.
  See more than one person
  in different types of
  situations.

- **Water.** Continue dating.
  Spend time together and
  apart. Talk and learn about
  each other.

- **Fertilize.** Add romance.
  Do special things. Buy
  cards and flowers, spend a
  night out on the town, etc.

- **Transplant.** Change;
  adjust to each others'
  needs.

- **Weed.** Communicate and
  change unwanted behaviors
  or beliefs.

- **Prune.** Keep inside the
  boundaries of the
  relationship, or direct those
  boundaries.

Enjoy the harvest! Smell the
roses together!

GROW FOR IT!

> **When one door of
> happiness closes,
> another opens; but
> often we look so long at
> the closed door that we
> do not see the one that
> has been opened for us.**
>
> *-- Helen Keller*

Chapter Eighteen
Understanding Women

What Every Man Should Know About Women (It's Time to Ask!)

Understanding the opposite sex can be like reading Greek. After all:

- Why do women get so upset when men leave the toilet seat in the upright position?
- How do you handle a loudly ticking biological clock?
- Where do women get the shopping "gene" from?
- What should I do when I ask her if she's OK, and she answers, "I'm fine! Just fine!!" (and you know she's not). Or she says: "You should know what the matter is!"

First, realize that women are different than men. They have a different kind of logic. You wouldn't go to Italy and expect everyone to speak English. So, don't expect women to speak the same language as men.

For example: When a woman says, "Honey, when you get a chance, would you take out the garbage?" What she means is "Take out the garbage now!" (What's the logic? Women don't like to give orders. They want to be "nice" and cooperative while getting the results they need, and they wish other people would be that way, too.)

When she gets upset because you didn't take out the garbage right away, and you find yourself saying, "She said, 'When I had a chance,'" *remember:* she spoke in a different dialect. What she said is *not exactly* what she meant. It's like comparing Southern to Northern dialects, or American to British or Australian English.

In the same vein: Women don't understand the "sports gene," or why men can't stop to ask directions when they're lost. At some point, we all must realize that we're different, accept it, and make it work. If you know that a woman loves to shop, make sure you tell her how wonderful her new outfit looks on her. Then, she can let you watch your favorite sport in peace!

Responses to frequently asked questions:

1. The Toilet Seat Issue:
Why do I have to put it back down?

A. Majority rules. There are more women than men, so put the seat back down when you're through.

B. A woman's environment is very important to her. To a woman, a raised toilet seat looks "ugly," "tacky," and "disgusting."

C. A forgotten toilet seat is a sign of disrespect to some women, and to others it means you don't really care. Think about it. After all, you may have never run into the bathroom in a hurry, only to find yourself sitting in a bowl of toilet water.

D. Men frequently miss the "mark" when aiming. (As a woman, I have never been able to understand this since men have something to aim with and women don't!)

E. If you can't find a good reason in this list, just accept it for what it is. Women don't want to grab a potentially wet seat and put it down. And most women figure men could learn to aim better, being the sportsmen that they are! However, in men's defense: For years, boys' mothers yell, "Put the toilet seat up!" This is what little boys hear in potty training. They're rightly confused when, all of a sudden, the rules change, and women want them to do the opposite! So ladies, be tolerant. It took a long time for your man to remember to lift it up, so please forgive him when he forgets to put it back down!

2. Biological Clocks:

"What should I do when my girlfriend mentions how much she'd like to have kids someday, and I'm not ready to talk about it?"

A. Mistake number one is to ignore the statement. Next time, she's sure to say it louder.

B. Respond in a non-emotional way, i.e., "Yep. . . although I'm not ready yet for the responsibility of children, I can sympathize, since almost everyone has that as a goal." If she persists in talking about it, you could say something like: "That's a pretty serious subject. Can we discuss it later?" Or try to change the subject. Ask her if she's bought anything special lately, or offer to take her shopping. Ask, "Do you want to go out to a movie?" (By all means, avoid seeing "Three Men and a Baby!") If this issue is emotionally charged, you may want to get her interested in something else. This will give you time to prepare for a more effective discussion later.

3. "I'm fine! Just fine!" and. . . "You should already know why I'm upset!"

A. If you've forgotten something important to her, she'll remind you with a similar statement. Of course, you should be able to read her mind, right? After all, didn't they teach mind-reading in high school?

B. First say: "I'm sorry you're upset. Please tell me about it." It helps to admit you've done something wrong, even if you think it's a minor offense. Women really appreciate men who are strong enough to be humble and who ask for forgiveness for their part in any mis-understanding, i.e., for-

getting to call or for-
getting a birthday
(even if the oversight is
non-intentional).

C. It's *much* easier for
women to let go of the
upset if you acknow-
ledge that there is one
and that you want to
help.

4. Shopping "Genes"

A. Don't try to understand
it, just accept it.
B. Don't try to change it,
just accept it.
C. Don't try to hide your
money in a shoe box
under the tree, Al
Bundy-like. She'll find
it!
D. Don't try to understand
it, just accept it.

**5. Why do women get all
dressed up to attract
men, and then get upset if
men really look at them?**

A. Don't try to understand
it. Just let it happen.
Secretly, they're
pleased you noticed.
But, they can't let you
know that, because

their friends might
think they're
"naughty."

B. They don't want you to
interpret the way they
are dressed as a come-
on. Think of it as just
an "attention-getter."
C. Go on a subliminal
Flirting Safari™ with
someone who has
flirting skills you
admire. Observe them
and learn to say the
right things to people at
the right moment.
Begin to recognize the
subtle tips that say
someone's interested in
you.

> **There was a definite
> process by which
> one made people into
> friends, and
> it involved talking to
> them and
> listening to them for
> hours at a time.**
>
> **-- Rebecca West**

Top Ten Ways to Win Women Over When You Screw Up.

10. When you mess up a flirting line, smile at her and ask for a second chance, or give her a compliment. "Why is it that the more attractive a woman is, the more ways my mouth finds to embarrass me?"

9. If you call her by the wrong name, try saying something like: "OOPS, I just called you by my favorite aunt's/sister's/ teacher's name," or "You remind me of a Janet I once knew." Or try smiling sheepishly and just say you are sorry. (Careful — you don't want to over-apologize. . . it could make you look more guilty.)

8. If you climax too soon, hold her close for at least 20 minutes. . . stroke her hair and whisper in her ears. You can find other ways to make her happy.

7. If you forget an important event (birthday, anniversary, etc.): Give her a gift every day for a week to celebrate each year or decade that you've been together. Make it up to her now or you'll be paying for a long, long time. For forgotten birthdays, celebrate in small ways for a week; i.e., flowers one day; take her out and have the piano player at the local establishment play the birthday song or one of her favorite songs, send a belated birthday card each day for a few days, and include a short note about some quality you like or appreciate about her.

6. If she asks you to write a love letter and you send an erotic one (very bad move!): Try to save face by sending a letter that makes no reference to sex - tell her what you like about her mind, her looks, the fun you have together. If you want to include a sensual message. . . send it separately or minimize it so you won't be accused of having only one thing on your mind.

5. If you accidentally burp in front of her, her parents, or friends: minimize the damage by just saying "Pardon me." Skip the cute jokes.

4. If you can't remember where you parked the car: Be a knight in shining armor - don't make her walk around and around the parking lot. Usher her to somewhere safe and bring the car to her.

3. If you forget to open the door for her and she's standing there waiting for you: Say "Allow me," and motion her through the door. Try also saying "After you," and usher her in.

2. When you're late, admit it. Stop at a pay phone and call her.

1. If you're lost - Make her realize how unique you are. . . . ask for directions!

Chapter Nineteen
Managing Your Emotions
The Straw That Broke the Camel's Back

Before you snap, before you say, "That's it! I'm not going to take it anymore!" or, "Never again!" find out how you can prevent the volcano of emotions from erupting.

Why is it that some people seem to have abundant patience and good will, and others have short fuses? Did you ever wonder why sometimes you seem so tolerant of life's challenging moments, and other times feelings overwhelm you and cloud your ability to cope with even minor events?

NLP (Neuro-Linguistic Programming) can explain much of that, and teach you how to use positive and negative feelings and emotions to benefit you. It gives you skills to put you in control of your life.

Imagine a time when you snapped and said, "That's it! I'm not going to take it anymore!" You probably took action right after that. Maybe you told someone just how you really felt. Or maybe you quit your job, ended a bad relationship, or stopped smoking. This is what we call **getting to "threshold."** It can be helpful or detrimental, depending, of course, on the situation. If you get mad at your boss, lose your temper, and get fired on the spot, getting to threshold does not produce great results.

Remember a time when you said something that you shouldn't have. You quite likely let all the little events build up until it became too upsetting. Create new choices and avoid those high-intensity times by trying the following:

Ask yourself this question: What did you do immediately before you snapped? Did you imagine all the times your boss/boyfriend or family did whatever they did, over and over? As you remembered these events, did you find yourself getting more and more upset? Good! Now that you know how this happens, begin noticing the specific type and order of these feelings of upset. You can prevent emotions from building up until you explode unnecessarily and end up having to apologize, if you pay attention to these cues.

In a relationship, little events can build up and create a background of emotional tension. So, if nothing is ever said or done about these events, or if we withhold the necessary communication to make our partners aware of the problem, the mere act of forgetting to take out the garbage, the rapping of their toothbrush on the sink, or the perpetual pantyhose all over the bathroom could put you in orbit!

Prevent yourself from getting to "threshold!"
Act to prevent blow-ups! Be proactive!

One business owner used this technique to discover how many unfulfilled, repeated requests it took him before he blew up. His number was three, which meant that if someone made three errors in a day, did not complete three tasks, or if he had to ask three times for something before it got done, he knew he could end up being out of control of his emotions. This information is helpful to know about your boss or any other person in your life. Children are very good at knowing how far to push people before they really get in trouble. We could all learn from children!

One woman, whose abusive boyfriend would slap her, was able to effectively use the following techniques to end the relationship quickly and effectively. She learned to use her own "threshold" patterns to her advantage. That is, she learned how she normally creates and builds the upsets, lies, or irritating events up in her mind so they *boil*, and then she created a pleasing image of the future and how it would look when she handled the challenge.

She then imagined her boyfriend continuing to hit her, over and over and over, until she created a picture of her face so damaged it was unrecognizable. Then she said: "Never again!" with emotion. She imagined a better life without him (which is the key for the process to work), and was able to end the relationship in one phone call. Some people will let others abuse them 20, 40, even 100 times, or live with someone in pain for 10 to 20 years, before they reach their "threshold" and actually do something about it.

Here's a simple version of how the process works. Try it on your own. Remember, "threshold" is different in different situations (family relationships, work relationships, etc.).

The Threshold Process

1. Imagine a time when you were fed up with certain people or events. Think of a time when you had had it, and it was time to do something about it.

2. Freeze or slow down the thoughts, pictures, or sounds in your mind. What did you do? What do you notice?
   A. Did you see a "movie" of all the past events and add to it the current event? Did it seem real close? Were the noises loud and screaming?
   B. Did you take one event and blow it out of proportion? Notice what you do so that you can use it later.

3. Hear yourself saying your favorite anger words, i.e., "That's it! Never again!" Use the same forceful tone of voice.

4. Create and feel the possibility of all the good that you'll experience by changing your actions. Picture what your future will be like once you've handled this situation.

5. Take the appropriate actions.

Okay. You've had it. That's it. It's over. Never again! Follow these steps to find your threshold. Use it to prevent blow-ups, by taking appropriate actions and learning about yourself.

**Repeat the process again as many times
as it takes to get the desired effect.**

Top Ten Ways to Please a Man

1. Give at least five compliments a day. (Never combine them with any criticism.)

2. Compliment him in public.

3. Never, never criticize him in public or in front of friends.

4. Make him home-cooked meals!

5. Spend a night at home when you would prefer to go out.

6. More intimate relations (sex).

7. Fewer headaches.

8. Give him his private time and space.

9. Dress sensuously for dinner.

10. Give him the day off from mowing the grass - hire the neighbor kid.

Top Ten Ways to Please a Woman

1. If she usually does more household chores, give her the night off. Make dinner and clean the dishes.

2. Take the garbage out before she asks.

3. Wash and wax her car.

4. Hire a maid service.

5. Tell her how special she.

6. Never make her feel guilty for not having sex.

7. Make sure she gets plenty of foreplay, hold and cuddle her when it's over (20 minutes minimum for each).

8. Once in a while, don't roll over and fall asleep.

9. Be extra nice to her mother. (That means don't complain when you find out she's coming over for dinner.)

10. When she's upset, just listen — no advice-giving or problem-solving.

Top Ten Worst Things to Say to a Woman

10. You sound/act just like your/my mother (or my ex-wife).

9. You're nagging again.

8. So what's the point? Or, get to the point!

7. Come on, come on, let's go already!

6. This place is a mess!

5. Do I have any clean underwear?

4. You whore, slut, etc.

3. I'm just a paycheck to you.

2. You never want sex.

1. I DON'T WANT CHILDREN.

   OOPS! I forgot one: You take too long to climax.

Twelve Vocabulary Words That Men Should Use

It is imperative that men create new habits now by substituting the words below for the generic words "**fine**," "**okay**," "**nice**," or "**good**," when a woman asks how she looks. Men tend to use these neutral words and women end up frustrated because they feel they are not getting a real answer.

You look:

1. Terrific!
2. Fabulous!
3. Gorgeous!
4. Beautiful!
5. Exquisite!
6. Incredible!
7. Sexy! (Use only when she is dressing to please you.)
8. Hot!
9. Irresistible!
10. Stunning!
11. Enchanting!
12. Glorious!

Women: Try to understand that men prefer to remain neutral when giving a compliment. However, guys, it is best to err using the above words rather than "okay" or "fine."

Eight Short Phrases Intelligent Men Use

1. I'm sorry.
2. What can I do to help?
3. Let's go out for dinner.
4. It's my turn to do the dishes.
5. I hired a housekeeper.
6. I'm here for you.
7. Thank you for. . .
8. I feel. . .

Chapter Twenty
Re-Invent Your Relationships!

**What if the purpose of your relationship
is truly in your hands?**

**What if it's up to you to create them
and recreate them every day?**

Try re-inventing the person you're with. Imagine him/her to be the "ONE" (At least for now). Imagine coming home from a long day at work knowing that your significant other will soon be there for you, and you will both be there for each other.

Lavish attention on your partner, and remember to listen — really listen — to what s/he is saying. Be considerate of woes, make him/her "right," and give at least five compliments during the evening. (This exercise is worth trying!) Ask each other to create unconditional acceptance in which you nurture and support one another. Try this in the beginning of a relationship, in place of the usual "checking out," and watch it grow!

So what if he wants to veg out in front of the TV, as long as there's enough room on the couch for both of you, and you have a great book to read or a Walkman to listen to — especially if he's massaging your feet! We all feel more giving when others give to us. Learn to ask for that foot massage, and remember to tell him/her how great it feels.

Our lives are filled with joy as well as stress. Remember to continuously re-create the purpose for your relationships. Do this every day, sometimes minute-to-minute. A great movie to illustrate this idea is "House Sitter," with Goldie Hawn and Steve Martin. In this movie, one person does the work, then the other person does the work, and eventually both work equally at creating a great relationship. The movie, although a little farfetched, etches the message that "your relationships are in your mind."

When you think of someone, that is the relationship. Who you imagine this person to be is who s/he is for you. Charming, hilarious, sweet, sensitive, etc. All the wonderful, special qualities s/he had in the beginning of the relationship are always still there, but if your mind thinks of him or her differently, s/he can become annoying, cutesy, dumb, humorless, moody, etc. Same person, different assessment.

In order to reinvent the relationship, decide that's what you want to do. First, are you loving the right person? In the right ways? (Read Barbara De Angelis' book *Are You the One for Me?* to find out.) Once you've decided to reinvent, do it all the way! I truly believe that there's someone for everyone out there. Take seminars and seek new resources/ammunition to get what you want in your current or future relationships.

**While one person hesitates because
he feels inferior, the other is busy
making mistakes and becoming superior.**

-- Henry C. Link

Chapter Twenty-One
Mastering Your Relating Skills

No one ever said that relationships were easy, but we would like them to be. You either find yourself complaining about the SOS (same old stuff) in a relationship, or about how hard it is to meet someone worthwhile. Some people get to the point where they just give up and find happiness in being alone. Others simply get crazy and try advertising for a mate on a billboard! It seems that our choices are limited to either putting up with the "stuff" in a relationship, or choosing to hit the road for other pastures.

The problem is this: People grow accustomed to certain ways of being in a relationship: doing certain things together, being comfortable enough to stay home and "veg out," having a certain level of understanding and/or misunderstanding. If you decide to hit the road, you know you'll be starting all over again with someone new.

It will be some time before you get to the "comfortable" stage. That's also when we start noticing all those little things that get under our skin. This is when all the best qualities of your boy/girlfriend seem to become their worst!

Scenario 1: Your boyfriend is so "nice." He's always helping people. In the beginning, what really attracted you was how helpful he was to you and even to complete strangers. Now that you're in a relationship, your expectations have changed while his qualities and habits remain the same. His niceness drives you crazy, because he's either:

A. Late for your dates because he was helping someone on the freeway with a flat tire, or. . .

B. Helping a friend on the phone who was upset, etc. Meanwhile, you sit at home waiting for some quality time together. When he does arrive, you fume. He can't understand why you're upset (which only makes matters worse). His rationale is that he was only trying to help someone. You're still upset and go on and on about how he's "done it again!"

Scenario 2: The "martyr" does for everyone else, but gets nothing in return. The martyr complex has predictable symptoms. For one, martyrs keep score. Every wonderful act scores them a point. They think subliminally, "If I'm nice to everyone, they'll automatically know what I want, and will give it to me." As time goes on, the score gets higher, and the martyr finds remarkable ways to make you miserable. (Expect recounts of all the things done for you so you'll feel miserable and guilty and immediately give this person exactly what they want). Of course, martyrs will also tell you that they never really wanted to do the things that they previously agreed to. They call it "personal sacrifice." They only did it because they cared so much about you. This is also the time when they let you know that since you aren't doing what they want, then you must not care about them as much as they care about you. (Another point!) They demand that you prove how much you care by taking action.

1. Don't let your significant other play another round of victim/martyr. **Break the pattern** by playing a different game. Otherwise, you'll end up as another John and Marcia, "lovingly complaining to others about how much you care about each other and how perfect your life would be if only s/he would change this one thing."

2. Each time the SOS happens (same old stuff), recognize that this is not acceptable to you.

3. Never condemn this person, or say, "There you go again."

4. Ask your significant other a startling question. Change the subject. Or tell a joke. Do anything! Just don't overreact, and don't get "plugged in."

5. Try translating the complaints they have.

   From: "You always leave your pantyhose all over the bathroom."
   To: "I guess my pantyhose get in the way. Where do you want me to put them?"

From: "You never bring me flowers!"
To: "I'm questioning the relationship right now and I need a sign from you that you still care: flowers!"

6. Encourage the martyr/victim to be responsible for what s/he wants. Ask straightforward questions, and wait for an answer. You could say something like, "So what you really want is. . . ?" Or, remind him/her, "Please make sure that this is something you really want to do, because if you agree, then you're not allowed to say, 'I didn't really want to do this.'"

7. You'll feel much better taking positive action. But don't expect immediate results. Change takes time.

There are so many ways to make a difference in new and old relationships. Keep in mind, however, that there are times when it's best to end the relationship. How do you know? When the risks/benefits of leaving outweigh the risks/benefits of staying.

**Truth is such a rare thing;
it is delightful to tell it.**

-- Emily Dickinson

ℜelationship ℑnsurance
ℑop ℑen Ways to Avoid the Crash & Burn of a ℜelationship

These tips can save you lots of money on marriage counselors as
well as countless hours of grief:

1. Read relationship/self help books and listen to audio-tapes alone
    and together (minimum three per year). Practice what you learn.
    Suggested reading (although there are many books available, I
    suggest trying these first):

- *Creating Your Life Relationship by Relationship* - Susan Bradley.

- *Making Love All the Time; Secrets About Men Every Woman
  Should Know; Are You the One for Me?* - Barbara De Angelis.

- *Why Men are the Way They Are; Myths about Male Power* -
  Warren Farrell.

- *Tough Love* - Doctor Dobson.

- *Men are from Mars, Women are From Venus; Mars and Venus in
  the Bedroom; What Your Mother Couldn't Tell You and Your
  Father Didn't Know* — John Gray.

- *How to Make a Man Fall in Love With You* (for men or women,
  but skip the first part about the "bastard trap"; I do not encourage
  male bashing) - Tracy Cabot.

- *Unlimited Power; Unleash the Giant Within* - Anthony Robbins.

- *Hot Monogamy* — Dr. Patricia Love.

- *Romance 101; 1001 More Ways to be Romantic* - Gregory Godek

- *Love Notes for Lovers* - Larry James

- *101 Nights of Grrrreat Sex* - Laura Corn

- *Secrets of Sensual Lovemaking* - Tom Leonardi

- Any other positive thinking book.

2. Take seminars:

- Loving University's "Creating Your Life-Relationship by Relationship" and Dating, Mating & LongTerm Relating™ series.

- "Making Love Work" - Barbara DeAngelis (available on video).

- "Men are From Mars, Women are From Venus" - John Gray.

- "The Men we Never Knew," — Daphne Rose Kingma.

- "Mastery University" or "Unlimited Power" - Anthony Robbins.

- "Light His/Her Fire" - Ellen Kriedman.

- "The Power of Love - The Art of Conscious Loving (Tantra)."

- "Basic Sensuality."

- "Communication Course" - Landmark Education.
  (We constantly update our lists on available and new seminars, so call us at 216-521-LOVE.)

3. Take romantic get-a-ways (minimum 3-4 a year)

- 3-day cruise.

- Check into a ritzy hotel for the weekend.

- Visit Niagara Falls.

- Spend a weekend in a cabin in the woods.

- A day at the spa together.

- Kidnap him/her for the day (ask your friends for help in arranging this).

- Take a mental health day from work, play hooky and do something fun together (once a year).

- Attend a weekend seminar on health, relationships, etc.

If you think you can't afford any of the above, ask your lawyer how much a divorce costs.

4. Take all those tests found in magazines like "Cosmopolitan," "Glamour," "Complete Woman," etc. (You'll learn a lot about women.)

5. Take care of your health, body, and dress appealingly for your mate on a daily basis, not just lingerie at night. Men, wear some sexy boxers for us.

6. Romance each other daily and flirt often.

7. Create a *Treasury of Memories* - buy a journal to log your thoughts and emotions of special times and paste in all the special memorabilia.

8. Write monthly communication letters to each other. Listen to a gripe s/he has and take action on it.

9. Praise and thank each other 12 times a day.

10. Touch each other often (a kiss a day keeps the lawyers away!).

Hint: Put this list on your refrigerator and remind yourself to take action on each one.

Chapter Twenty-Two
DO IT NOW, Procrastinate Tomorrow!

How long have you put off cleaning your basement, writing that thank-you note, doing the laundry, going to the dentist, or doing your taxes? These are just a few of our everyday acts of procrastination. But what about the biggies?

Now try this on: Don't ask for that raise. Don't go on vacation. Don't diet or start your own business. Don't create that perfect relationship. Want to stop? Read on.

Fear stops us from taking action. Procrastination is a fear: fear of the consequences of our actions or dread of an everyday task. Dread, furthermore, is a fancy word for fear. Those of you familiar with Neuro-Linguistic Programming know that our self-talk and the wording we use affect how we feel. For example, would you rather "communicate" with someone or "confront" them? We often avoid "confronting," and procrastination sets in. The minute something becomes a "confrontation" it takes on a negative connotation. Change the word to "communication" and it seems more pleasant. The minute our brain hears the word "confrontation," the adrenaline flows, blood pressure goes up, and we turn around and run. Call it a "communication," and you'll feel calmer and approach it more quickly.

Change your feelings about a task that you're now procrastinating about.

1. Change the wording, i.e., how you describe it to yourself and others. Don't label. Don't say: "Changing jobs is risky," or "I'm only exchanging old problems for new ones." Try calling your new position "a new opportunity for more pleasure, challenges, and money, which all lead to more satisfaction." Don't call starting a new relationship the "same old same old." Call it experiencing the thrills of intrigue, intimacy, and more!

2. Create a pleasant picture in your mind of yourself actually completing the action. Also — and this is very important — see yourself doing it with a big grin on your face. *Fake it 'til you*

make it. Notice how good it feels. You believed in yourself! You did it! Keep in mind that thoughts about doing something are often more frightening than actually doing it.

3. Paste a smile on your face. It really does help change the way your nervous system responds to the task!

Now if you want to procrastinate, go ahead, procrastinate. It's a personal choice. But remember that while waiting to do laundry until you have no socks to wear, you exchange one procrastination/fear for another. Fear of having to wear dirty socks replaces the procrastination of avoiding laundry (which I term *laundritis*: fear of having to spend time lifting clothes and detergent instead of lifting iced tea while enjoying your favorite TV show). Some people don't balance their checkbooks because they don't want to know how little they have left. Don't worry. If any of these examples hits home, smile now, and realize you're human. However, if any of these fears are limiting your life — stopping you from moving to a warmer climate, accepting a better job, or not allowing you to find satisfying relationships — then remember:

The fear of the unknown subsides once action begins. A decision to begin action is necessary. The main element in procrastination is lack of convictions or goals. Your problems show up only when you lose sight of your goals. Note: Don't be conventional and follow others. Have your own goals. Remember: It's not your responsibility to worry about what others think of you. Honor yourself and make a commitment to change, whatever it is. Begin NOW!

Nothing is terrible except fear itself.
-- Francis Bacon

Chapter Twenty-Three
Peak Performance States:
Or, Feeling Great When You Need To!

Use the following exercises to overcome feelings of fear and apprehension over possible rejection in social situations. As you read this, remember how you felt this morning when you woke up. How many times did you hit the snooze button? How groggy did you feel? Did you feel really rested? How many cups of coffee did it take before you were well on your way?

When was the last time you woke up fully refreshed, extremely alert, and ready to go? It felt great, didn't it? These two paragraphs may have already had you experiencing different feelings and thoughts. You are beginning to realizing how easy it is to change the way you feel. You'll begin now to use the modern science and discipline of Neuro-Linguistic Programming (NLP for short) to create peak performance states — and learn when you need them most.

Let's prove it. In the following exercise, you will create a stressful feeling and then effectively get rid of it. It's easy, and as you'll see, we do it all the time.

1. Imagine that you're stuck in a traffic jam with nowhere to go, and you're already late for an important meeting. On a scale of 1 to 10, how frustrated are you? 11? How are you breathing? What are you saying now? How tense are your muscles? How high is your blood pressure? How fast is your heart beating?

2. Now, R-E-L-A-X. Take a deep breath, and let it out, blowing all the stress away. Notice how much better you feel. Shake out your arms to release any left-over tension. Good. Feel better now?

Consciously, you knew you weren't stuck in traffic. It wasn't happening right then, but your brain created a physical reaction in your body. Frustration and stress never reduce a traffic jam. It's better to accept the situation, accept that you'll be late, relax, and plan your strategies. This way, when you do get there, you'll be more effective and calm. If you really can't stand to just sit and "do nothing," while in traffic, consider keeping a notepad in the car to organize your thoughts for a meeting, or jot down things to do.

Notice how effective you can be at changing how you feel. Learn ways to create a strong peak performance state. Imagine that your body is a robot and your brain tells the robot what to do, see, and feel. Now picture yourself holding a juicy yellow lemon. Pretend you're cutting a slice of this juicy lemon to eat. As you put it in your mouth, taste it. You are probably salivating and/or making a sour face. Yet there is no lemon! Your brain told your body there was a lemon, and it reacted as if there was one really there. So. . . if your brain told you, the robot, that you're feeling very loved right now, and you imagined what that would look like, feel like, or sound like, wouldn't you start feeling more loved? Of course!

Remember a time when you felt very confident. You felt like you had all the time in the world to get a job done. Every time you looked at the clock, you were surprised by how little time has gone by, and yet how much you'd done. You smiled and noticed how good it feels to relax, breathe deeply, and have plenty of energy. That's the kind of energy that has no limit, and you feel as if you could tackle anything at any time.

Now, if you want to feel this good before asking someone on a date or discussing a touchy subject, try the following exercise:

1. Stop whatever you're doing.

2. Take a deep breath, exhale, and shake out your arms.

3. Remember what one of your peak performance moments feels like. I.e. (feeling like you have all the time you need to get something done, or like everything you touch turns to gold.)

4. Notice: that your robot is doing and feeling what the brain told it to do.

5. You should now be in a peak performance state. Yeah!

6. Repeat the process over and over, often enough so that it becomes habit and very easy to feel.

7. If you want to create this response even faster and easier, or you have difficulty really feeling the peak performance states, call us for some extra tips, and consider contacting an NLP practitioner so you can learn with experts.

Picture your life a month from now, at a time when you'll have already mastered this technique. You'll be able to turn stress off, and turn productivity and good feelings on. The quality of your life will go up, up, UP! What will you be able to do in one month, that you aren't doing now, if you learn this skill? After one year? Five years? Write those results down on the list below, and call us with your successes!!

SUCCESS LIST:

1. _____

2. _____

3. _____

4. _____

5. _____

6. _____

The thing I fear most is fear.

-- Michel Eyquem de Montaigne

Top 17 Worst Things to Say to a Man

1. Why don't you stop and ask for directions?

2. Do I look fat to you? (Don't put him in a difficult spot: He has 3 choices-tell you the truth, make you feel better, or blame PMS.)

3. How do you feel about kids?

4. So. . . when are you going to: cut the grass/take out the garbage/ finish painting the. . . _____?

5. Please put the toilet seat down !

6. Did you forget where the hamper was?

7. You sound or act just like my/your father or my ex-husband.

8. I have a headache tonight.

9. You men only want one thing/have a one track mind.

10. You're not going to wear that are you?

11. You're so chauvinistic.

12. Your dinner is in the oven!

13. I'm going home to my parents.

14. What did you do/say that for?

15. You always/never. . . (fill in the blank).

16. Can we talk? (He thinks that he's going to blamed for something.)

17. You're just commitment phobic.

Chapter Twenty-Four
Before it's Really Over and
Another Relationship Bites the Dust

Is it over? Time to say NEXT? Another relationship cast away?
What happened? What did you learn from it? Do you really know all
the facts? Answers to these questions are very real to you. But guess
what! There may be another way to interpret what happened.

Have you heard, "I'm just not getting back what I put into this
relationship," or, "I never get what I need to be happy," and "It seems
to be a one-way street"? Don't feel bad if you have heard or said
these common complaints. Sometimes we just cannot give to others
what they seem to need. The reason for this is that many of us have
not taken the time to really figure out exactly what we need to feel
totally loved. Some people need to be told and must hear how much
they're loved; nothing else will satisfy them. Others need to be taken
out and sent cards and gifts just often enough to get the message
across. Others need personal contact (hugs, being together, touching).
(These people develop a "disease" I jokingly call "skin hunger," where
it's just not enough to be in the same room with a partner; they need
to be at your side.) If you don't share the same needs, you won't
understand why your partner feels the way s/he does.

You might assume that if you could communicate with each other,
in a bottom-line manner, your specific need — and then give your
partner enough of what s/he needs — everything would be just fine.
But guess again! Just when you thought you had the secret, more
information comes along. **Beliefs and value systems can interfere.
The rules we grew up with also affect our relationships.** Imagine
how two people would get along if one were taught to never raise his
or her voice during a disagreement, and the other grew up in a family
that valued screaming it out to the bitter end!

Example: Julie and Andrew came to my office totally frustrated and
on non-speaking terms. Their relationship was great until they
stumbled across conflicting rules and beliefs. They were at a party
when Andrew decided he had had enough. Julie had spent "too much"
time talking to another man, so he interrupted her by saying, "Julie, we

need you over here." When Julie realized that Andrew interrupted her solely to get her attention, she was angry. Her rule? You never interrupt a private conversation. Andrew's rule? When you attend parties *together* you stay *together*, and any other behavior is an insult to the person you go with. But Julie believed parties were social occasions and people were meant to split up and mingle.

Their beliefs and rules contradicted each other. Yet each believed themselves to be right. When they realized that these rules and beliefs were learned since childhood, they negotiated on their party rules to allow more freedom for Julie and more togetherness for Andrew.

Seems simple, right? But it works. Learn to recognize when rules, beliefs, and values get in the way of a great relationship. Listen for phrases that include words such as *should, always, must, never,* and *if.*

Examples:

- *If* my girlfriend really cared, then she would *always* be honest; she would *always* notice when I don't want to go out; and she would *never* spend money recklessly.
- A great boyfriend *always* understands when I need to spend time alone.

The trouble with these rules are: We don't know how that person defines "honesty"; we expect a mate to know telepathically when to leave us alone or when we want to stay home; and, we don't know what spending money "recklessly" means.

Ask these questions in the beginning of a relationship:
1. What *should* a boyfriend/girlfriend *always* do?

2. What *should* a girlfriend/boyfriend *never* do?

3. Ask specific questions about the meanings of words, i.e., how would you know when I am being *honest*, etc.

Ask the above questions now, before trouble brews.

ᘓop ᘓive ᘓips on ᘓaying Goodbye

1. Say: "Let's just be friends. I would prefer not to get romantic at this time." Men hate this one because they "know" what we mean by this. Try to maintain a platonic friendship, but only if the other party is emotionally ready to do this. Give people time to adjust.

2. Write a letter stating the qualities you like about this person and why you'd prefer not to continue the relationship. Share your real reasons; for example: I'm not ready for a relationship right now; I don't feel we have enough in common; I don't think we're looking for the same things in a relationship; we aren't compatible enough; I'm looking for someone who wants a family; we're too different; I haven't healed from my last relationship; I'm going to try to make it work with my last girlfriend or former wife; I can't give a relationship the time and energy it deserves right now, etc.

Examples:

Dear Jane,
I've had a great time getting to know you. We've laughed a lot. The more I get to know you, the more I realize how special you are and that you are looking for someone special to complete your life. There are many reasons I would want to be your friend, but I do not see a romantic, intimate future for us. So if you can and still want to, let's remain good friends. Good luck on finding Mr. Right.

Dear John,
I noticed how much it means to you to have a love interest in your life. I believe dating is kind of like using the remote control on the TV. Dating different people is like checking out a channel. Some channels you watch longer than others until you decide you only want to stay with one channel. I'm not ready to be in a serious

relationship right now and prefer to continue dating other people.
We can continue to date casually or maybe we should break it off
to prevent either of us from getting hurt.

3. Leave a message on their voice mail or answering machine when
   you know they won't be home. It may be less courageous than
   talking to them in person, but it sure beats the alternative of not
   answering the phone or refusing to return messages.

4. Allow the other party to vent their feelings as long as they do not
   become abusive.

5. Always end relationships before they become explosive. One man
   I was dating came up with a list of things that bothered him about
   me by the third date. After listening to the laundry list, I evaluated
   his complaints and realized that they were past issues stemming
   from problems he had had in his marriage. This man needed to
   have more time and space to heal before continuing relationships.
   I explained to him that if he already had a problem with so many
   little things at this early stage, we'd be better off not having a fourth
   date. He didn't particularly like what I said, but he did respect me
   and the decision.

   Pay attention to the little red flags that show up either on the
   phone before you meet someone new or on the first few dates.
   Always end your dating relationship when you notice major
   incompatibilities.

Nothing is so much to be feared as fear.

-- Henry David Thoreau

Chapter Twenty-Five
When it's Over, is it OVER?
Knowing When to Hold and When to Fold

**I'll think of some way to get him back.
After all, tomorrow is another day.**

*-- Margaret Mitchell
Gone With the Wind (1936), pt. V, last line*

You've been through it all before. You know s/he isn't right for you, yet you hang onto a relationship that is marginally alive or hopelessly miserable. Why aren't you getting what you need and want in this relationship, and why aren't you able to give your partner what they need and want? Why do you keep hanging on, your mood swinging back and forth from hopeful to depressed? You say to yourself, "My partner will change, want to spend more time with me, and begin to be what I want him/her to be." Meanwhile, the other party is thinking, "When is s/he going to understand that I'm not ready to commit, and that I don't want to change?"

Relationships can be so unequal. One person can be totally in love and the other barely interested. Why can't two people fall in love with each other at the same time? Quite often we want what we can't have. If someone is temporarily unavailable, they become even more desirable. Hence, people play the cat-and-mouse game. Playing cat-and-mouse can work for healthy relationships. But what about people who constantly find themselves attracted to the wrong people (i.e., someone who is angry, married, commitment phobic, etc.)? If you're one of "those" — or even if you're not — take this survey:

Cat-and-Mouse Survey

1. Do you sit waiting for phone calls, or alternate between avoiding calls and desperately waiting for them?

2. Are you alone on birthdays and holidays?

3. Are you rarely included in his/her group of friends or relatives?

4. Do you spend 2-3 days per week in despair over this relationship?

5. Does s/he break commitments with you often?

6. What are the top three top things you'd like to change about this person?

7. Do you vacation together?

8. Do you help each other out with household chores (i.e., yard work, fixing things, decorating)?

9. In public, does your partner act proud to have you as a companion?

10. Do you see each other (when possible) at least 50% of each weekend, and at least once during the week?

11. Does s/he enjoy your children? (Answer only if this applies.)

12. Does s/he criticize you or your decisions often?

13. Are you often disappointed by this "SPECIAL" someone?

> **Questions 1-5:** If you answered "yes" to two or more, you may want to consider ending this relationship.
>
> **Question 6:** Look at your three answers to this question. Can this person realistically change these things? If not, here's another sign it may be time to move on.

Questions 7-11: If you answered "no" to even three, you may need assistance in understanding why you would choose someone who really isn't there for you.

Questions 12 & 13: Answering "yes" to either of these questions is enough for you to stop now, and truly consider what you have in common. Ask yourself, "How am I benefiting from this association?"

If you know from the above answers that your relationship may have been on shaky ground for some time, but you really can't see how you can "give up" this person, it's time to address another problem: separation anxiety. If you're willing to put up with a lot of emotional upset just to be in this relationship, be aware you're in for long-term suffering.

You have most likely developed an unhealthy pattern in this relationship, and possibly in past relationships, too. So this pattern must be BROKEN — now, NOW, *NOW*! If you don't break this pattern, you may never have what you really need, want, and deserve in this area of your life.

If you now know that you must end a relationship, prepare yourself. Read the book *How to Survive the Loss of a Love*. Seek the help of your friends and family, a therapist, or relationship coach, to help you break this negative pattern and get out of a relationship that doesn't give you what you need. Plan some fun events with old friends. Ask a friend to write a singles ad for you. Answer a couple of personal ads; it's a great learning experience. People who advertise tend to state what they want or don't want in a relationship (in a non-threatening way). Or join a dating service.

You deserve to find, give, and receive love. You spend a lot of time with your career; now it's time to spend it on your love relationships. Heal yourself. Have fun with your relationships, and break your negative patterns. Find someone special who will share your life.

> This above all: to thine own self be true,
> and it must follow as the night the day,
> thou canst not then be false to any man.
>
> -- *Shakespeare*

> Basically my wife was immature. I'd be at home in
> the bath and she'd come in and sink my boats.
>
> -- *Woody Allen*

> Cras amet qui nunquam amavit
> quique amavit cras amet
> (Tomorrow let him love who has never loved
> and tomorrow let him who has loved love).
>
> -- *Anonymous*
> Latin Pervigilium veneris (c. 350), refrain

> To love and to be loved is the greatest happiness of
> existence.
>
> --*Sydney Smith*

Chapter Twenty-Six
Love: Playing the Game...
And Winning!

Going all the way!

If you haven't had a relationship with someone and wanted to say "Let's go all the way!" then it's time. If you have a partner right now, a newer one or someone you've been with for years, you need to look them in the eyes and say "Let's go all the way!" Go all the way and play the game full out.

Many people come to me to get permission to start really living their lives. Their relationships have turned into flatliners, or they never felt that they were really in love with the person they married. You'd be surprised at how many people marry the first person they dated. Then they wonder, 25 years later, if they did the right thing. They fantasize about dating. Most of you fantasize about what married life will be like with the perfect person. I say that unless you are willing to go <u>all</u> the way with someone, you will never be happy in that relationship.

So, go all the way in creating trust, openness, a true partnership, and loving honesty. Go all the way in exploring your beliefs, your passions, and totally supporting each other's dreams and goals. Go all the way in exploring your sexuality with each other. Spend time living outside your comfort zone with each other. Risk making daring statements of your love and affinity to your significant others.

If you were in a jet flying in for a landing and you noticed that it was going to crash, what would you write in a note to your loved ones? Write this now and send it to them. Or better yet, call them up and tell them. Don't let fear of embarrassment or rejection stop you from expressing your loving concern and feelings for someone. Go all the Way!

Let every upset that you resolve in a relationship be a marker for the miles you'll travel together in life. Go all the way to create a new understanding with each other. Be committed to each other. Experience the sacredness of allowing yourself to be intimate only with one person in your life. Take joy in knowing that this one person and one person alone...knows you in a way that no one else ever will.

Know that with this person you will share something very private, loving, and healing: your self, your body, your mind.

Going all the way means exploring every new resource that will make you more loving, forgiving, more joyous, playful, happy, self-expressed, and wise. Don't let a moment of your life be wasted by upset, hatred, jealousy, negative thinking, or worry. Do this by looking for the silver or gold lining in every mishap that life brings. Share your life with someone who will be there for you, even when you can't be there for yourself. Go all the way to believing that there truly is an irresistible partner waiting out there for you. He or she is watching, waiting, are scratching their chin, wondering where you are and what is taking you so long. Go all the way, every day, to being better today than you were yesterday. Turn over every nook and cranny to find your beloved or have him/her discover you. You can do it no matter where you are right now on your path in life.

Every forward step you take will bring you closer. Every moment spent in growing and healing will take you closer to a profound love. Never give yourself deadlines to finding love..give yourself alivelines instead. Live to live grace-fully, grate-fully, and great-fully. I trust that you will be more tomorrow than you are today. I trust that you will fall down and pick yourself up many times along the way. I trust that you will achieve all that you want if you keep on going. Games in relationships? But isn't that what we try to avoid? You say, "I don't know why I have to play games just to have a relationship," or "If I need to do that to have a relationship, count me out!"

We all grew up playing games. Even as babies, we dropped our bottles and waited to see how many times mom/dad would pick them up. Perhaps you'd run to the top of the stairs as fast as you could so mom could have a heart attack and rush to your rescue. You learned at a young age how to get the reactions you wanted, and playing games was fun, fun, fun!

Life is a game. Do you want to play? Do you want to love? Do you want to be loved? Wait: did your parents give you the "Encyclopedia of Relationships"? What? Didn't that Relationship Encyclopedia salesman knock on your door selling the latest version?

Love is like playing hide and seek, riding a roller coaster, tipping a seesaw. Love can seem like a game of Scrabble or Monopoly, chess, or a booby-trap! Love can act like any assortment of games. Why? Because **you** make the rules! Your past experiences could throw you into a game you don't enjoy playing. For example, the abusive parent or the alcoholic can reappear in your relationships over and over until you resolve those issues. Get support in dealing with your past. Attend self-help seminars, find and read books dealing with your personal issues, and spend time discovering yourself.

I suggest you view love and life like a seesaw. Sometimes, you're up in the air; sometimes you're down on the ground. A seesaw also gives you control: sometimes, you put your mate in the air. (Remember "Farmer Brown, Farmer Brown, won't you let me down?") Sometimes we love it, and sometimes we hate it.

When will **you** control the seesaw? When you learn to use your weight and when you realize it's your turn, you'll have the control you need. Relationships need the cat-and-mouse syndrome, the chase and retreat, the ebb and flow. The sun comes up and then goes down. Tides come in and go out. What goes up must come down.

Life is boring when it stays the same! Sure, it seems safe. But try this. Get on that seesaw again and pretend that you're on the bottom looking up. **You** now have all the control. **You** can make that person on the other end happy or miserable. **You** can surprise them when **you** let them down quickly. Or, **you** can monopolize the situation, and never let them down. A word of caution here: monopoly or control may feel good and create a level of safety for a while, but it never fulfills love.

Ask yourself: What will happen when I relinquish control, and I'm up in the air? How will I feel? Do I trust my partner? Do I need to? If the seesaw operates properly there will always be moments of perfect balance: the kiss that seems to last forever, words that remain in our hearts and souls, the look of love, the dreams, the feeling of "melting." There will be moments when you're up in the air not knowing exactly what to expect, trusting innocently and praying it will all work out. Love is created through these moments, moment by moment.

There are times when love flows up and down, and up and down, so effortlessly, and other times when it takes all of your effort to tolerate the situation. You may not want to try again. You may want to leave. It may not feel as much fun anymore. Look at the "seesaw" in your life. Where are you? Where is it? How fast is it going? Are you both having fun? How long do you keep each other in the air? How long is each of you on the ground?

Balance occurs in a relationship when partners take turns. The one exerting the most interest and effort, takes a break and is rewarded by having someone chase after them for a while. Example: He chases you for a while, then you chase him. Just before he seems bored, you feign indifference and allow him to chase you. Marriage sometimes creates stalemates. The seesaw stays motionless and boring. Each person experiences fear. Each is afraid to upset the balance. Meanwhile, the seesaw rots away from non-use.

Balance is like sailing, tacking right and left until you reach your destination. It's like a pendulum on a grandfather clock: each swing to the right swings back to the left.

It constantly shifts back and forth, passing by on the

left   then   middle   then   right

Try saying the following words slowly out loud, or at least to yourself. You will notice something interesting.

left middle right
right right right
left left left
middle middle middle
left middle right
left middle right
right middle left
right middle left
right
right
right
right

Right now, you're probably wondering "Why am I reading this? What does this left-middle-right stuff have to do with anything?" This is ----- (you fill in the word)!

OK. Let me demonstrate. Feel the next few lines.

left
left
left
left
left
left
left
left
left

                  middle

                                      right

Notice, that you begin to feel better here because the pattern has resolved itself.

Again:

                  middle
                  middle
                  middle
                  middle
                  middle
                  middle
                  middle
                  middle
                  middle
                  middle
                  middle
               stuck in the middle

                                right right
left left

Notice the feelings you have as you read along. Where is the tension? When do you notice an internal, quiet, and subtle feeling of

relief when it changes again, and balances out? These patterns occur
in all of our relationships.

Start becoming aware of patterns, and you'll recognize, and stop,
potential relationship killers. Relationships "die" when there is too
much or too little of any one thing. Too much sex, not enough money.
Too much niceness, not enough niceness. Little or no understanding,
too much understanding (and lack of challenge). The relationship dies
because it is taken for granted, much like the air we breathe, or the
number of times our hearts beat in the time it takes to read a page.
Love is a game. Life is a game. Your family and career are games.
My question is this: When will you accept the game and begin playing?
When will you come out and play? Or are you going to take your
marbles home forever because you might not win?

Please come out and play! Don't stay home alone! Don't give up!
Begin to create a world that includes love. Let there be love on earth
and let it begin with you!

Love, is the wild card of our existence.

-- *Judith Ray*

Continue to read and re-read this book. Use this book. Share this book. Do something — anything — differently than you did yesterday! Keep finding and re-creating the successful parts of your relationships, while you improve the inevitable flaws. Above all, keep trying, period! You won't write a loveless obituary at the end of your existence. Be able to say "I loved well and often."

Good luck on your journey. Believe in yourself. Give to yourself. Heal your wounds. And BE love itself.

Love alone is capable of uniting living beings

in such a way as to complete and fulfill them,

for it alone takes them and joins them by

what is deepest in themselves.

-- *Pierrre Teilhard de Chardin*
1881-1955 French Paleontologist

P.S. You're not done yet . . .

There's a Companion Guide and the Love Directory to have fun with. If you've been implementing what you've been reading , then you should definitely be more irresistible. If you have not purchased the companion guide as of yet, call 1-800-Compatible (1-800-266-7284)
or send $14.95 plus $3 shipping and handling to
Loving University Press at P.O. Box 771133, Cleveland, Oh 44107.

Don't forget that there is also an 80 minute audio tape on
Love & Attraction Strategies that will help you understand & use them more.

Tis better to have loved and lost
Than never to have loved at all.

-- *Alfred, Lord Tennyson*
In Memoriam (1850), 27. st. 4

There is only one happiness in life,
to love, and be loved.

-- *George Sand*
Letter to Lina Calamatta
(March 31, 1862)

When love and skill work together
expect a masterpiece.

-- *John Ruskin*

Hell, Madame, is to love no longer.

-- *Georges Bernanos*
Le Journal d'un Curé de Campagne
(The Diary of a Country Priest)

Directory of Love Advice

Use the following lists for quick, practical solutions and insight on delicate matters of relationships. Because I believe that laughter can be the best medicine, some of the advice is designed to make you laugh and lighten up. Use the lists to get through the tougher moments of your journey through

Dating♥Mating♥LongTerm Relating™.

Top Ten Sexual Turnoffs for Men

10. Nagging.

9. Too much or not enough makeup/hairspray/perfume.

8. Bad breath.

7. Talking about your yeast infection.

6. Talking about your headache.

5. Foul vaginal odor and taste - wash and rinse well.

4. Large baggy underwear and mumu's. (Men love lingerie at any age.) Note: Matching undergarments that say you're special are a must even under your gardening clothes.

3. Not wiping well and/or leaving bits of toilet tissue.

2. Body hair - underarm hair and leg stubble (unless your hair is soft by nature and light in color.)

1. Talking about how good your last lover was.

ꝺop ꝺen Sexual ꝺurnoffs for Women

10. Treating her like a "cheap" date.

9. Not listening to her.

8. Nerdy clothes (no brown or plaid shirts, goofy sandals with black dress socks, "holy" socks).

7. Body odor - including buffalo breath.

6. White cheesy material in the genital area - clean that "thing" before every encounter (smegma is definitely out).

5. Toenails that are dirty or too long and ragged. (Watch fingernails, too!)

4. Not enough foreplay - get her ready guys! (45 minutes minimum.)

3. Dandruff and greasy hair - don't use too much conditioner.

2. Not wiping well and body acne (see a specialist).

1. Loud burps and farts during or just following sex. At least excuse yourself.

    (I know I said ten but I couldn't forget these two!)

11. Dirty sheets!

12. Soap and dirt scum in and around your bathroom sink, toilet and bathtub.

Top Ten Pet Names for You-Know-Who

Men have told me that they name their anatomy so a complete stranger isn't making 90% of their decisions.

1. Sir Winston

2. Harry and the Twins

3. "Him"

4. Peter's Pride

5. Monsieur

6. The Lone Ranger

7. My Pal Joey

8. Mr. One Eye

9. Mr. Happy

10. Dr. Love

Runners-up

11. Mr. Excitement

12. Mr. Wiggly

13. Willy

14. Trail Bologna

15. Winky the One-Eyed Wonder Lizard

Top Ten A.K.A.'s for That Time of the Month

Unlike men, women do not usually name their genitals. However, menstruation is an exception.

1. Aunt Flow is coming to town.

2. The Monthly Visitor.

3. "I've got my you-know-what."

4. Monthly Friend

5. Strawberry Daiquiri

6. It's Midol time again.

7. "I'm on the rag." (I personally despise this one.)

8. "That time of the month."

9. The curse.

10. My period.

⟨op ⟨en ⟨ntros to the ⟨afe ⟨ex ⟨alk

1. If you haven't had a vasectomy, what kind of birth control do you suggest?

2. Did you bring any condoms? (One woman I know jokingly calls them condominiums.)

3. I made us an appointment (pause then add. . .) at the AIDS Testing Clinic.

4. I'll show you mine if you show me yours (AIDS card!).

5. Unless my heart and mind are connected to the person I'm seeing, I'm not interested in sex.

6. Most relationships end in the first three months. . . so I prefer to wait for sexual intimacy.

7. I haven't had any unwanted children in my life and don't plan to start now. What type of birth control should we use?

8. How do you feel about children? Well, I wouldn't want to see any little Johnny's or Susie's running around, so let's be smart and protect ourselves.

9. I know that you feel pretty excited right now, but how excited would you be about changing diapers?

10. Have you ever:
    Visited an AIDS Hospital Ward?
    Supported AIDS Research?
    Lived Dangerously? (This is a real conversation starter.)

Top Ten Ways to Recognize a One-Night-Stand *in Advance*

1. Too many compliments.

2. Sexy kisses that last too long (usually longer than 5 seconds with no breathers.)

3. He starts making comments like: "I'm tired; it's such a long drive home. Do you mind if I sleep on your couch?"

4. He seems to know all the right moves to wear away your resistance.

5. He tells you that it's been ages since he's had sex. (Hint: it's just long enough that you feel sorry for him and feel like it's safe.)

6. He begins to caress you, which seems innocent enough to begin with but you start to enjoy it.

7. Even though you draw the limits his caresses, he'll find other ploys to keep you involved, i.e., more compliments, telling you how sexy you are, acting like a little boy ("Oh, just touch me for a little bit, it's been so long, you don't know much this means to me.")

8. He says, "Trust me!" or "Let's just sleep next to each other. That's all." Or, "I've never felt this way/haven't felt this way about a woman in a long time."

9. He suggests you put on your flannel pajamas so that you'll trust him a little more but he continues to caress you.

10. You're seduced on one of the first 3 dates and he never calls you. **Note:** It's still a one-night-stand even if you're seeing each other for three months, decide to be intimate, and then he never calls again.

Top Eleven Ways to Avoid A One-Night-Stand

1. Get very intimate with these three words: No. . . No. . . NO!

2. Don't invite him in for coffee.

3. When he tries to touch the forbidden zones, take his hand and move it back to his body.

4. Repeat #3 as often as necessary. (If he doesn't get the hint after 2-3 times, really exaggerate the movement and give him the "I-mean-business" look or say, "Please get this hint.")

5. Button up your blouse all the way, *change your body language,* sit in a less relaxed position, back straight, and legs together.

6. Explain that you do not want to take things so fast. (He may consider this a challenge, so back up your statements.)

7. Make sure the location of the dates is not conducive to having sex, i.e., agree to meet him and drive your own car; be careful about doing dinner at his house; if you have dinner at your house conveniently arrange for friends to drop by; pay your ex to visit (just kidding), and plan commitments like, "I'd invite you in but I have to make a call by _____ time and it will be a long one."

8. Say "no". . . a lot more.

9. Wear a T-shirt or button that says "What part of NO! don't you understand?"

10. When nothing else works and if he persists. . . unzip his pants. . . peek in and say, "With that little thing?" It works every time.

11. When he asks, "So, how do you like your eggs in the morning?" Respond : "Unfertilized."

Top Ten Ways to Make Yourself Feel Better If You Had a One-Night-Stand

1. Immediately begin looking for another fish to fry. You won't concentrate so much on the one who didn't call if you have three more prospects vying for your attention.

2. Confess all to your best friend.

3. Send him one of these notes:
   #1 Hi, _____. You were great in bed but I found someone better. Sincerely, _____.

   #2 Hi, _____. Great sex! Just wanted you to know my AIDS test was positive. Sincerely, _____.

   #3 Hi, _____. Sorry I haven't heard from you. Just wanted to suggest a good doctor for herpes. Just a hint: If you take l-lysine the painful lesions will go away faster. Sincerely, __.

   #4. Hi, Please give me a call. My doctor finally figured out the virus/rash I have. Sincerely, _____.

4. Promise yourself to never have another one-night-stand.

5. Keep your promise.

6. Try to remember that not all men are lower than pond scum (just the ones who didn't call).

7. Eat chocolate, lot's of it. (Go shopping or just pamper yourself.)

8. Imagine him on a date with Mrs. Bobbit.

9. Imagine #8 again.

10. Send him a copy of the movie "Fatal Attraction."

Top Ten Seduction Strategies

1. Begin seduction in the morning with an extra long kiss goodbye if you are living together or call your partner at home just to say how special they are.

2. Call and try to convince him/her to leave work early and meet you at a hotel or for a special lunch. (This one can only be done if you are already in a relationship.)

3. Dress in a very appealing, sensual way.

4. Walk and talk confidently whenever you are near your mate.

5. Touch lightly while looking deep into eyes.

6. Touch lips with your pinkie finger-slowly trace the outline. . . then stop and look into eyes.

7. Kiss the tip of your finger then press your finger onto the center of lips.

8. Stroke hair gently while breathing soft sigh into ears.

9. Start at top of head and massage every body part except the genitals.

10. Stop touching for two minutes and wait for other party to respond. Imagine someone doing this to you and you'll understand why it works so well.

Top 13 Ways to Tell if You Are a Great Lover!

1. You spend time exploring every nook and cranny of each others bodies.

2. You have eye contact while making love. Say, "Look at me," or "Look into my eyes."

3. You are willing to try new things in bed.

4. You are comfortable making noise and expressing your pleasure.

5. You don't make your partner wrong for their fantasies.

6. You do not rush your partner and would never complain that they are taking too long.

7. You cuddle after making love.

8. You utilize sex as an expression of love, not just a physical release.

9. You realize that it's okay if she chooses not to climax.

10. You realize that he can have a soft-on instead of a hard-on and still be horny.

11. You understand that a man likes his penis to be caressed and loved sometimes gently and sometimes firmly.

12. You realize that a woman must be thoroughly aroused and comfortable with you before you touch her vagina.

13. You realize that women need and want to be reassured while you make love. Whisper in her ear, tell her that you have all night, that you are "there" for her, encourage her to go for it, and hold her close to you while you caress her.

Dear Reader,

The book you have just completed is a sampling and collection of *Dating, Mating and LongTerm Relating™.* By the time you complete it, you will have learned many new skills, and are very likely already experiencing relationships with more savvy, fun, and optimism. Remember that relationships are real, changeable, growing things, that need constant attention. One book can't provide everything. See my forthcoming books for more information on each topic:

- Flirting with Greatness
- Between a Man and a Woman
- When Women Speak in Estrogen & Men in Testosterone
- The Art of Dating ♥ Mating ♥ LongTerm Relating™ (Vol. 2)
- The Journey into Love
- The Secret of Creating Your Life--Relationship by Relationship

You can receive sneak previews of each of these books by subscribing to Loving University's On-Going Relationship Correspondence Courses. You'll receive a chapter a month and phone support from our team members. Future chapters may be from any of the these books. You'll begin mastering relationships and learning new skills to make you feel more confident and happy about relationships. *Plus,* you'll have advance notice on upcoming events, seminars, and audio- and videotapes

All for only $22.95 per year.

Keep adding to your book, and get the latest update in new relationship technologies. **Future topics include:**

- How to Know the Difference Between Loving Someone and Being "In-Love."
- Letting Go — Knowing How and When to Do It

Send your check or money order to:
Loving University, Press
P.O. Box 771133
Cleveland, Ohio 44107
Or call 1 (800) Compatible (1-800-266-7284) to register by phone.